The N[...]
Book of Places

Edited by
Joseph Harker and Paul Howlett

theguardian

ATLANTIC BOOKS
LONDON

Published in Great Britain in hardback in 2005
by Atlantic Books on behalf of Guardian Newspapers Ltd.
Atlantic Books is an imprint of Grove Atlantic Ltd.

Copyright © Guardian Newspapers Ltd 2005

The moral right of Joseph Harker and Paul Howlett
to be identified as the editors of this work has been asserted in
accordance with the Copyright, Designs and Patents
Act of 1988.

The Guardian is a registered trademark of the
Guardian Media Group Plc. Guardian Books is an
imprint of Guardian Newspapers Ltd.

ISBN 1 84354 457 1

A CIP record for this book is available from the British Library

2 4 6 8 10 9 7 5 3 1

Designed and typeset by Patty Rennie Production, Portsoy
Printed in Great Britain by Mackays of Chatham plc,
Chatham, Kent

Guardian Books
Ormond House
26–27 Boswell Street
London WC1N 3JZ

The *Notes & Queries*
Book of Places

Joseph Harker and Paul Howlett edit the
Guardian's weekly Notes & Queries column.

Contents

Foreword   vii

British Places   1

Places Overseas   53

Natural Places   141

Mythical and Mysterious Places   185

Odd Places   255

Foreword

Remember when it used to be said that everyone should know their place? Thankfully, times have moved on; but can you imagine all those people who didn't know where their place was, but were desperately trying to find it? If only this book had been around then. Whether one's place was on cloud nine (or indeed clouds 1–8), somewhere on route 66 (though you never can decipher the place names in that song), or on top of the world's highest mountain (which constantly seems to be getting higher and higher), this book would have been the ideal place to start looking.

But, even today, many of us often feel out of place, and the chances are that wherever we're trying to find our place will be somewhere in this book. *The Notes & Queries Book of Places* brings together the combined wisdom and knowledge of over fifteen years worth of *Guardian* readers' questions and answers. Since the 'Notes & Queries' weekly column was launched in the paper back in 1989, it has received tens of thousands of contributions, from some of the millions of readers who stretch to all corners of the globe. In the early years, before the internet, the column was the best place to find the answers to all those annoying everyday questions that stick in the mind until, well, you think of something more interesting. But even in the Google era the questions still keep coming. They are the sort that the search engines just can't answer: why are boxing rings square? How big is the sky? Who lives at Number 9 Downing Street?

Like its companion volume, *The Notes & Queries Book of People*, we've divided this compilation into handy sections. Starting close to home we have 'British Places', answering crucial questions such as: what exactly is traditional 'English' culture? Or, when did the first 'Disgusted of Tunbridge Wells' letter appear? And where is the one-eyed city?

'Places Overseas' will help you discover if you can still cross the Rubicon; where in the world has the highest standard of living; and, if it wasn't constructed in a day, how long did it take to build Rome? In 'Natural Places' we look at the Earth, the sea, the sky, and beyond: which place on earth feels the hottest? How do they measure the height of waves at sea? And just what is the universe expanding into?

In 'Mythical and Mysterious Places' our focus is the unexplained: what ultimately became of the Mary Celeste? Why is there no M7 motorway? Where will it all end? And why does nothing in my house work properly?

Of course, some questions simply defy categorization, so we've picked an eclectic mix for our 'Odd Places' chapter. Where is the oldest place with 'New' in its name? Which clockface is seen by the most people? Where was the first semi-detached house built, and does anyone know where the second one was?

So whether in your back garden or some mystic wonderland, at the Earth's core, or out beyond the stars, we're sure you'll find your own ideal spot in the following pages. And when you do, we very much hope that you'll give this book its own special pride of place.

Joseph Harker and Paul Howlett

BRITISH PLACES

In the Olympics we are Great Britain, yet in some other international events we are the United Kingdom. How is it decided which to use for each event, and would I be eligible for this competition if I were from Belfast?

Britain referred to itself as 'Great Britain' up until 1945 and the 'United Kingdom' thereafter. This was so we could sit next to the US in the UN Security Council. Therefore, in events that started before 1945 – the Olympics, the Davis Cup, the Ryder Cup (before we competed as Europe), we compete as Great Britain. For more recent ones (such as the Eurovision song contest), we compete as the UK. As to Northern Ireland – I don't think it matters in this context. You could argue that pre-1945, we were ignorant of Ireland's role in the UK. You could also argue that post-1945 we have become lapdogs of the US.

Antony Belling, Norwich

If you were from Belfast you could compete for the UK in either type of competition as Great Britain is a misnomer – in these competitions we should use the Olympic team name 'Great Britain and Northern Ireland', commonly abbreviated to GBNI. If all that is too much hassle, you could take advantage of the British–Irish agreement, which allows anyone born in Northern Ireland to claim Irish nationality and just compete for Eire.

Gary Dunion, Edinburgh

In the light of the resurgence of the Welsh and Cornish languages, what was the last native language of the UK to die out before these were spared the same fate?

Cornish was never actually spared that fate as its last native speaker was Dolly Pentreath, a resident of Mousehole, who died in 1777. Modern Cornish exists only due to revival attempts, and comes in several versions. Manx Gaelic's last native speaker, Ned Maddrell, died in 1974 but again that language is being revived through scholarly effort. The last language to die out in the UK to be lost altogether may, therefore, be Cumbrian, which was a Brythonic Celtic language spoken in and around Cumbria until the eleventh century.

Sean Palmer, Brighton

Norn, a descendant of Old Norse spoken in Orkney and Shetland, died out sometime in the eighteenth century. I don't know if you can say it died out completely though, as many words in the Orkney and Shetland dialects are still derived from Norn.

Danny Farquhar, Thurso, Scotland

Are Scotch eggs really Scottish?

The practice of encasing a pre-cooked egg in forcemeat developed not in Scotland but in North Africa. The technique made its way to Britain via France and was first recorded in England during the reign of Elizabeth I. Scotch eggs were originally spiked with cloves and highly spiced in an attempt to sweeten the often putrefying meat. The term itself is obscure but may come, though I doubt it, from a corruption of the word 'scorch' (which in Elizabethan times had ribald associations). The first Scotch eggs were cooked over a naked flame, after all. For more about Scotch eggs and Algerian cookery see Colin Cutler's excellent book, *1001 Strange Things* (Beaver Books, 1970).

Ali Mignot, London SW1

Scotch eggs originated in the Whitby area of Yorkshire in the late nineteenth century. Originally they were not

covered in sausage meat but in a rich, creamy fish paste
before being sprinkled with breadcrumbs. Their name in
those days was 'Scotties', allegedly because they were
made at an eatery by the name of William J. Scott & Sons
close to the seafront. Hence, over a period of time, the
term Scotch eggs was adopted. This was thought to be
because the major foodstores who started selling the del-
icacy were unhappy with the name and adopted a more
formal approach to marketing. Sausage meat replaced the
fish paste purely for packaging reasons, although on my
last visit to Scarborough the original recipe was still
being used in a local cafeteria. More information can be
obtained from *Culinary Delights of Yorkshire* by Peter Bone
(R. Fyfe & Co, 1981).

Robert Egan, Stevenage, Herts

According to *A Caledonian Feast* by Annette Hope (Grafton
Books, 1989), Scotch eggs were an Indian export in the
early nineteenth century, along with curry and kedgeree.
The dish was first mentioned by Meg Dods, *c.* 1830, in
one of her recipe collections. Hope continues: 'It bears an
odd similarity – striking though probably coincidental –
with an Indian dish called *nargis kofta*, which consists of
hard-boiled eggs coated with cooked spiced minced mut-
ton and fried, then cut in half and served in a sauce of
curried tomato and onion' (p 251).

Lynda Bowen, Nottingham

When did the first 'Disgusted of Tunbridge Wells' letter appear in a newspaper? Why was he/she disgusted?

I seem to recall that this was used in letters of complaint by Jimmy Edwards in the old *Take It From Here* radio programme.

Rita Kiernan, Nailsea, Bristol

The expression might have something to do with Dr William Webber, who caused the 'Webber Riots' in the town in 1864. He complained to the Home Office about a drain – see my book, *Royal Tunbridge Wells: A Pictorial History* (Phillimore, 1990).

Roger Farthing, Tunbridge Wells, Kent

The editor of the *Female Tatler*, which first appeared in July 1709, asked her readers to send her 'the ridiculous things that happen at Epsom, Tunbridge and the Bath'. In August she referred to a letter from a lady in Tunbridge – 'a place resorted to by Persons with a Design to be as ill-tempered and censorious as they possibly can'. Among such persons, it appears, were Lady Carper and Mrs Undermine.

Helen Mead, Oxford

In chapter five of *English History 1914–45*, A. J. P. Taylor states: 'The passport was, of course, required by foreign governments. British citizens do not need a passport to leave this country in peacetime or to return to it.' Is this still the case?

Yes, A. J. P. Taylor was right, one can leave the UK and return without a passport – although strictly speaking this does not apply if one is flying. Clause 42 of Magna Carta states: 'Any freeman may travel abroad without let or hindrance of the King and return safe and secure by land and by water except in the time of war.' I know this because several years ago our son found his passport was out of date late in the day before he was due to go on holiday with his girlfriend. The Public Records Office looked it up for me and explained that France, his destination, could refuse to let him in, but in July at the height of the holiday season the French authorities probably would not notice his passport was out of date. I was advised, however, that he should have on him the above Magna Carta clause, in case his exit from or re-entry to this country was queried with an out-of-date passport.

(Mrs) V. M. Crews, Beckenham, Kent

British citizens aren't citizens as such but only subjects of the Crown and we do need the permission of the Sovereign to leave the country – otherwise we might all leave to avoid unpleasant wars and taxes and the like. Rather than take up her time writing letters allowing her trusty and well-beloved Waynes and Traceys to spend their fortnights in Ibiza, the Queen provides these passport substitutes. If you don't want to carry one, you could petition the Queen for a leave-giving letter, which might make quite an impressive travel document.

Humphrey Evans, London, N7

In 1973 I travelled from Heathrow to the Netherlands without a passport. I had quite a job to persuade the UK emigration officer to let me out of the country but he let me go reluctantly after I asked him if he could quote an act of parliament requiring British citizens to have a passport (I was sure that there wasn't one). The appropriate Dutch official, a member of the police force, when told I had no passport merely smiled and said welcome to the Netherlands.

Herbert Layton, Gloucester

Some years ago a French immigration officer, after studying for a few moments the passport my husband had handed him, remarked quite politely that it was difficult to believe he was only ten years old. My preoccupied spouse had mistakenly taken not his own but our younger son's passport with him on this solo journey; embarrassed and dismayed, he began apologising and explaining, but had hardly

begun before the officer stamped the passport and handed
it back to him with a shrug – a Gallic shrug, no doubt.

Merivan Coles, London SW5

**I keep hearing claims of this or that town/city
having the most number of pubs per head of
population, but which one actually does?**

About five years ago I counted twenty-two in the small
town of Ennistymon in County Clare. With its last census
population of 920, this gives one for every forty-two
persons. Admittedly, several only opened at weekends and
others shared their trade with others such as the saddler,
florist, coal merchant and undertaker.

Barrie Pepper, Leeds

According to Whellan's directory of 1856, Newcastle
upon Tyne had a total of 446 public houses and 'beer
houses' for a population of 87,748. This works out at one
for every 200 of the population. But I imagine today
there will be many more people per pub.

W. Collinson, Belmont, Durham

The tale at Thirsk Racecourse transit camp 1944, was that
the town square had forty-eight pubs around it . . .

Colin Troughton-Smith, Selsey, West Sussex

There is a local Norfolk saying that Norwich has a church for every day of the week, and a pub for every week of the year.

Paul Stalham, London W11

Having spent the first twenty-one years of my life in Norwich, complete with shoe factories, heavy engineering, Colman's factory, Mackintosh's chocolates – all now closed – I would like to correct Paul Stalham. The correct saying was that Norwich had a pub for every day of the year, and a church for every week of the year – many more of each than Mr Stalham claimed.

Tony Friedlander, Colchester, Essex

I don't know. But people in Zagreb always claim their city has the largest per capita number of coffee houses in the world.

Christopher Gordon, Winchester, Hampshire

Is there anywhere in Britain where you can still buy a Saturday-evening sports paper? If not, when did they fall out of use?

Were the questioner to live in Nottingham, he could buy its *Football Post* every Saturday. It's 100 years old and still here, if less comprehensive than in the golden days when the rival *Nottingham Evening News* also published a *Football News* to hit the Saturday-evening streets. I read both avidly. The main value of provincial football *Green 'Uns* (or *Pinks*) was filling the gap between Saturday afternoon and Monday morning, when there was no television, no local radio and with national Sundays very selective in the games they reported.

Ralph Gee, Nottingham

You can still get the Sheffield *Green 'Un* each week. What is more, if they had won all the games that the paper says they were robbed of by the referee, the woodwork and bad luck, both United and Wednesday would still be in the Premier League.

Charlie Withall, Sheffield

I buy a *Pink* in Newcastle upon Tyne most Saturday nights. They are best read in the pub just after a game, although the lack of Saturday Premier games might be one of the reasons why many have closed down. There is also *The Green* in Stoke-on-Trent. I think others have closed down because of Saturday-night publication of Sunday papers. Ceefax and the internet might also have had an influence on reduced sales.

Kevin Mochrie, Newcastle upon Tyne

I have before my very eyes a copy of the Portsmouth *News SportsMail*, with its proud and celebratory headline 'Giant step to safety' plastered over a photo of Steve Stone celebrating his goal: Pompey 1, Man Utd 0. Our first win over them since 1957!

Trevor Masters, Fareham, Hants

Ours, in the Southampton area, is called *The Pink* and is not only useful for checking had you seen the same match as their reporter, but is excellent for catching up on all the local sports news. Does anyone know why they are always printed on pink paper?

Paddy Browne, Salisbury, Wilts

For several generations Exeter has claimed to have the narrowest street in the country (Parliament Street, 24 inches at ground level). Is this so, or is it a case of local hopefulness?

The North Yorkshire coastal village of Staithes has an extremely narrow street – Dog Loup – which is sometimes claimed to be the narrowest in the country. A recent visit (albeit without tape measure) suggests that it could well be under 24 inches wide and therefore narrower than Parliament Street, Exeter.

Tony Gibbs, Bramfield, Hertford

This question raises issues of definition: what is a 'street'? Does it have to be named 'street'? Does it have to be used by the old legal category of 'passengers' going from one public place to another? Does it have to be maintained at public expense? Does it have to be marked on standard street maps?

The old fishing town of Whitstable in Kent has several ancient publicly maintained thoroughfares, marked on street maps, that link other public roads, and that are similar to or even smaller or at least narrower than Exeter's Parliament Street. The test they fail is merely that of nomenclature: they are, I believe, all called 'alley'. They include Beach Alley, Evelings Alley, Bonners Alley, Knights Alley, Reeves Alley and Kemp Alley. In the narrowest part of the smallest alley, users have to turn sideways and pull their tummies in; this street is called Squeeze Gut Alley.

George Hornby, Rainham, Kent

Munro's Tables list all the Scottish peaks above 3,000 ft in height. If sea levels are rising, at what point should mean sea level be redefined, and several Munros struck off the list?

Few things are simple when it comes to Munros. The first requirement here would be for the Ordnance Survey (OS) to redefine their sea-level datum at Newlyn. This is unlikely in the foreseeable future even though the de facto sea level might well be higher than this theoretical mark.

The second stage would be for the OS to apply this new datum to their maps, redrawing all contours and reducing every spot height by the difference between the old and new data.

The third stage would be for the Scottish Mountaineering Club (SMC), which has maintained the list of Munros since 1891, to ratify the new heights.

It is at this stage that the real complications start. The 3,000 ft mark converts to 914.4 m, so two hills could each be mapped as 914 m with one a Munro and the other not. Indeed Foinaven and Beinn Dearg, the two highest Corbetts (the next hill-category down from Munros) are mapped as 914 m. For a hill to be 914 m and a Munro makes it 914.4 m or (depending on whether rounding is up or down) 914.5 m, as 914.6 m would definitely be rounded to 915 m. This level of accuracy, even if available to the OS, has almost never been applied to its maps.

If the OS raised the datum by one metre, this would bring the three lowest Munros (Sgurr nan Ceannaichean, Ben Vane and Beinn Teallach, each 915 m) into the borderline bracket whereby more accurate figures would be required. Whether the SMC would be qualified to provide this level of confidence is debatable.

Dave Hewitt, editor, The Angry Corrie,
Cambuskenneth, Stirling, Scotland

Why is the 'Black Country' so-called? Is it because of the black soil in the area or is it because of the industrial revolution?

It is due to the pollution that coats everything black across the whole region. The small-scale metal-working perhaps caused more pollution over a larger area than, say, in the cotton towns. The same goes for the Charleroi area of Belgium, which is similarly called 'le Pays Noir'.

Nigel Barclay, Asse, Belgium

What is the maximum distance I can be from a Tarmac road in England or the UK as a whole?

What about Rockall? It's 300 miles off the coast of Scotland.

Justin Rigden, Adelaide, Australia

If you count as part of the UK the earth, magma, etc. that falls within in our boundaries, then technically it's that bit of the core of the Earth that comes under the UK.

Gordon Wilson, Reading

I imagine what the questioner wants to know is how far one can get from a road in mainland Britain. The truth is of course that nowhere where roads could be reasonably built remains free of them, so I am sure that you would have to look to a mountainous area. Somewhere in the middle of the Grampian mountains in Scotland might allow you to get twenty miles or so from a road of any sort but I would be surprised if you could get much further away on this overcrowded island.

Max Wurr, Stanmore, Middx

On motorway signs, a distance to London is shown. Obviously London is huge, so is there a specific place in the city that is used as a guide?

Traditionally, Marble Arch was used as London when approaching from the west. I believe that Charing Cross was used for distances from the south.

Patrick Russell, London

Things are similar in France. The distances to Paris are all measured from Notre Dame cathedral. There's a brass plaque on the floor about thirty metres in front of the church entrance showing the exact spot.

Steve Unsworth, Atherton, Lancs

What would be the right location for an English parliament?

Wall, outside Lichfield, lies close to the centre of England. It is also near the junction of the Roman roads running south-east–north-west (Watling Street, now the A5) and south-west–north-east (the Fosse Way – replaced by the modern A38). The site would therefore be a sensible place for an English parliament.

Martin Spiers, Glasgow

Well, since we had ours in London for 300 years, maybe we could try it the other way around. I reckon England's parliament should be in Edinburgh until 2300 and then we might think about letting England (and maybe some of the other 'regions') have a referendum on home rule.

Seth Chanas, Edinburgh

Washington?

Tom Sander, Leicester

Why does the word 'le' occur so often in the County Durham placenames: Hetton-le-Hole, Chester-le-Street, Houghton-le-Spring, even Hartlepool, etc.?

I always assumed that 'le' came from the old French *les*, meaning 'near', as in Carlton-le-Willows (Nottingham-shire), situated near the banks and willow trees of the

River Trent. This would also make sense for other places, as in Chester-le-Street, situated near the Roman road from Newcastle to the Tees.

Jenny Aitchison, Ruddington, Nottingham

Contrary to Jenny Aitchison's reply, there is no etymological evidence of the old French *les* occurring in English placenames. The 'le' common in placenames throughout the northern counties of England – not just Durham – is the French definite article.

In most cases it has lost the Norman French preposition that preceded it in the early Middle Ages (Chapel en le Frith, in Derbyshire – meaning 'chapel in the woodland' – is a rare case of it surviving). So the name Chester-le-Street places the settlement 'on the' (or 'by the') Roman road; Houghton le Spring defines it as 'belonging to the Spring family'; Poulton-le-Fylde establishes it 'on the plain', and so on. Hartlepool, which was variously written as Herterpol, Hertelpol and Hertepol in the twelfth and thirteenth centuries, is not related etymologically to the 'le' placenames.

Nick Mason, Evesham, Worcs

The name Poulton-le-Fylde – 'the community by the pool' – has no connection with Norman French. The suffix 'le Fylde' was added at the request of the townspeople in 1842 when, under the new postal service, letters were being delivered in error to another Poulton – now part of Morecambe. We became Poulton-le-Fylde and they Poulton-le-Sands.

Christine Storey, Poulton-le-Fylde Historical and Civic Society, Lancs

Why is Portsmouth called Pompey?

A lady, known throughout the navy as Aggie Weston, ran a hostel and club for sailors at Portsmouth. She used to give talks to them and attracted a large audience to the Sailors' Rest. It is said that in 1904 she gave a talk on the Roman general, Pompey the Great. She got very worked up about the reasons for his downfall, and when she told of his assassination one of the sailors called out: 'Poor old Pompey!' A few days later Portsmouth Football Club had a match at Fratton Park. They played badly, and when eventually the inevitable goal was scored against them a sailor in the crowd called out: 'Poor old Pompey!' Others took up the chorus. It became the good-tempered theme for the football terraces and soon attached itself to the town.

Reg Sanders, Alresford, Hants

Why are Arndale centres so named?

Arndale is derived from the first name of one of the founders of the firm, and the surname of the other: ARNold Hagenbach, and Sam ChippenDALE.

Simon Green, Park Grove, Hull

The Arndale company, founded in Bradford in 1950, was one of the first to specialize in shopping developments and the only one of any size not run from London. It began by developing small parades of shops in Yorkshire and neighbouring counties. Its first big operation was the redevelopment of Jarrow town centre in 1958. The story of this enterprise and the early work of the company is told in *The Property Boom*, by Oliver Marriot (1967). Chippendale fronted the operation, buying derelict pieces of backland close to existing shopping centres and nego-tiating with councils for partnership in comprehensive redevelopment. One of his major assets was his ability to exploit his Yorkshire background (born in Osset, a descen-dant of the well-known furniture maker) and his manner with local councillors. To quote Marriot: 'North country councillors were suspicious in their encounters with developers and estate agents from London. The borough treasurer of Jarrow spoke admiringly of Chippendale: 'He was a bit blunt and outspoken and he impressed some of my councillors who were more than a little difficult to impress. You see he spoke a language we understood.' And of course he made sure that his deals were financially favourable to Arndale – absurdly so in the case of Jarrow. Hagenbach, the minor partner, was a third-generation Swiss baker from Wakefield. After the war he sold his chain of baker's shops, although they continued to trade under the Hagenbach name for many years.

Peter Edwards, Senior Lecturer in Urban Planning,
Oxford Polytechnic

Arndale is an acronym for Architecturally Revolting Nonsensical Depressive Artless Ludicrous Eyesore.

Laura Scale, Prestwich, Manchester

What is the origin of the expression, 'sent to Coventry'?

There are two explanations. In the medieval period Coventry was an important venue for monastic estab-lishments: there were at least six within a five-mile radius of the city. In particular there was a silent order of Carthusian monks, one of only nine in Britain. They were granted land at Charterhouse, just off the London Road. If the London House had a monk among its brethren who found it difficult to adhere to the constraint of silence, the chatterbox was 'sent to Coventry'. There he would have his own small but detached cell, complete with workroom and garden, where silence would be a way of life rather than an imposition. The second, and certainly more pop-ular theory, concerns the Civil War and the Royalist Duke of Hamilton's Scottish soldiers, who were sent as 'prison-ers of war' to the parliamentarian city of Coventry. They were held in the disused medieval Bablak church (now the active Church of St John). As there was little chance of escape outside the city wall, they were allowed to walk around the town during the day. While the citizens did not treat them cruelly, they must have found their Scottish accents and different mode of dress more than a little strange, and preferred to give them a wide berth. This form of cold-shouldering thus led to the modern expression.

Lesley Pritchard, City guide, Coventry

Why do so few English placenames start with the letter J? If J is an unlucky letter for places, why is it not for personal names?

Most English placenames are of Anglo-Saxon origin but J (along with K, Q, V and Z) does not figure in the Old English alphabet: the letters were introduced after the Norman invasion of the eleventh century. Although many French elements are to be found in English placenames, it is no great surprise that non-native initial letters are not strongly represented. The one exception is K, which replaced Anglo-Saxon C in certain cases where the hard pronunciation was indicated.

Alan Clarke, Redland, Bristol

I shall soon be attending an international school in Hong Kong. A part of this will require me to display English culture, including national costume, songs, dances and recipes. Any ideas?

Join a Morris team. They may not be able to help with the recipes, but you'll certainly be able to learn some traditional English dancing, probably some English folk songs, and Morris kit is the closest you'll find to a national costume.

Sally Wearing, president, Morris Federation, Earlsdon, Coventry

The questioner should contact: the Centre for English Cultural Tradition and Language, University of Sheffield; the English Folk Dance and Song Society, London; the Folklore Society, London; any museum with a good collection of costume and an interest in traditional gear. For recipes, any large library with a good topographical collection, but do not discount the Women's Institutes and Townswomen's Guilds. National costume really doesn't exist, but regional, trade and local costume does.

Derek Froome, The Folklore Society, Hale, Cheshire

'English' culture perhaps existed between the departure of the Romans from the British Isles and the arrival of the Danes. Since then, England – which can only have a geographical meaning – has been under permanent foreign (British) domination. Our most famous rulers, Knut (Danish), Richard Lionheart (French), Henry VIII (Welsh), George I (German) and now the Greeks, have left the area of land called England without any culture of its own. We have no costume, songs, dances and recipes that have amused our British rulers and therefore been allowed to survive. Our language is a 'mish-mash' of Danish and French with just about anything else we can take on. Our national drink is tea – brought back by the British. Our ancestors were press-ganged into the British navy, conscripted into the armies, and died in British pits and factories to make the British owners rich. The Irish, Welsh and Scottish were further away from London, more protected by their mountains and sea. They still have a culture.

Andrew Moss, Greiveldange, Luxembourg

Sally Wearing may not be aware of the non-European origins of the Morris dance. J. A. Rogers, in his book *Nature Knows No Colour Line* (1952) cites a number of authorities to show that the name 'Morris' is a corruption of 'Moorish', and hence that the dance has an African origin. Dr Johnson's dictionary (1755), for example, has 'Morris

25

dance, that is Moorish or Morrice dance'. Shakespeare used the term 'Moor' to refer to all black Africans, as was the common usage since long before his time. The African origin of the Morris dance is further reinforced by the fact that, in times gone by, white dancers blackened their faces to dance it.

The main argument of Rogers' book is that there has long been a black presence in England – and in much of Europe – which has left many marks on our culture, including this, the most English of dances.

Charlie Owen, London N4

One traditional English dance might be appropriate. It requires twelve Englishmen, eleven clad in white and the twelfth in a white coat.

The dance starts with one of the eleven screaming at the man in the white coat. The latter replies by solemnly raising the index finger of his right hand. The eleven in white then leap in turn into the air with the man who uttered the initial scream, slapping hands and displaying unreserved ecstasy.

After one minute of this display, the eleven suddenly stop and begin to clap rhythmically, all the while staring into the mid distance. They are joined in the applause by the audience for approximately one more minute. The dance then ends.

This dance is called The Dismissal Of The Australian

Batsman (sometimes also called 'The Waugh Dance'). It is performed at most four times every five days during periods of the English summer.

Stuart Newstead, Oxford

Whatever happened to Fotheringhay castle, the scene of the beheading of Mary Queen of Scots? There is certainly a large mound still in existence but no stones, walls or any surface signs.

Fotheringhay castle has shared a fate similar to that of so many medieval buildings. The standing structure of the castle has been demolished, and only the defensive works – in the form of a substantial earthen mound and enclosing moats – are visible. This is the site of the original 'motte and bailey', and part of the moat of a subsequent larger bailey. The succession of stone and timber buildings, including a stone keep, chapels, a great hall and domestic buildings that once crowded these defences, were periodically demolished or altered before abandonment in the seventeenth century. Demolition followed and, according to the Royal Commission on Historical Monuments, by the nineteenth century the few remaining structures were pulled down by the owner, who used some of the salvaged materials in his own buildings.

Traces of former walls, floors and yards are still preserved below the turf, but only one visible fragment of limestone masonry, reputedly from a tower on the motte, is today visible, having been placed by the river earlier this century. Like so many other deserted medieval castle, village and manor-house sites across Northamptonshire, the medieval earthworks have proved far more durable than the buildings they were erected to protect.

Kim Lanning and Graham Cadman, Planning and Transportation Department, Northamptonshire County Council

What are the 'Lyme' and 'Lyne' that Newcastle and Ashton are 'under'?

Lyme was the ancient name of a large district on the uplands of the Pennine massif on the northern borders of Staffordshire, the south-eastern and eastern borders of Cheshire and the south-eastern borders of Lancashire. Not only does the name appear in Newcastle-under-Lyme and Ashton under Lyne (Asshton under Lyme, 1305), but also in a range of toponyms such as Lyme Park, Lyme Wood and Limehurst in Lancashire; Lyme Hall and Lyme Handley in Cheshire; Chesterton under Lyme in Staffordshire; and even in the final syllables of Audlem (Cheshire) and Burslem (Staffs).

The distribution of place names containing 'under Lyme' follows the 400 ft contour along the western edges of the Pennine massif, indicating that the Lyme was a region above this height.

The name Lyme is pre-Anglo-Saxon but is of disputed etymology. It appears to be either a derivative of the British word *lemo*, 'an elm tree', perhaps a British *lemia*, 'the district where the elm trees grow', or of a British *lummio*, giving Primitive Welsh *lim(m)* in some such sense as 'the bare or exposed district'.

The latter derivation would suit the appearance of the moors massif in modern times and probably its condition on the arrival of the Anglo-Saxons, who adopted the name from the Celtic inhabitants. However, a notable stand of elms in a region where any tree was rare could well have given rise to a district name based upon such a feature.

(Prof.) Barrie Cox, Department of English Studies,
University of Nottingham

Why is the Blackwall Tunnel under the Thames bent?

The first Blackwall Tunnel was built in the 1890s. It was constructed by driving from portals at the north and south ends, and also from two shafts close to the river. These four points are not in a straight line, so as the builders drove each section straight, there are sharp bends at the bottom of the shafts. This did not matter at the time, as only horse-drawn traffic and the occasional steam traction engines were on the roads; thus tight corners were not a constraint on traffic speeds. The second, east, tunnel was built in the late 1950s with curves to suit modern traffic conditions.

P. L. Sulley, C Eng, Yalding, Kent

A surveyor once told me that bends were built into the Rotherhithe Tunnel to prevent horses from bolting towards the light at the end of the tunnel.

Peter Lowthian, Marlow, Bucks

A Cambridge graduate recently claimed: 'Six of the twelve most important discoveries since the birth of Christ were made within half a mile of my rooms.' Assuming the claim is valid, what were the twelve, and which were the six?

If the 'importance' of a discovery is measured by the extent to which it altered the world, here is my list of twelve, none of which has very much to do with Cambridge: moveable type; heliocentric solar system; human blood circulation; electromagnetic induction and radiation; explosives; antibiotics; mechanical clockwork; telephony; vaccination; mercantile capitalism; digital computing; genetic inheritance and plant and animal breeding. You will notice, of course, that at least four of these were 'discovered' by people with close Scottish connections.

(Dr) Iain Stevenson, London WC2

Dr Iain Stevenson notes that 'none' of his list has very much to do with Cambridge. I disagree, as discoveries at Cambridge include: theory of gravity; DNA; atomic theory; Darwin's theory of evolution; digital computing; electricity and electromagnetic induction.

The other six discoveries were: heliocentric solar system; internal combustion engine; printing; mechanical clockwork; explosives; and antibiotics.

Douglas Ellison, London SE16

Douglas Ellison's list of six 'discoveries at Cambridge' is wide of the mark. Electricity: Galvani, Volta, Ampere, Ohm, Oersted and Franklin had no connection with Cambridge, or even England. Electromagnetic induction: the discoverer, Faraday, worked at the Royal Institution in London. Digital computing: Babbage was at Cambridge but produced no functioning computer, so could he really be the discoverer of digital computing? The credit seems really to belong to IBM at Harvard and Ferranti at Manchester. Theory of evolution: after three undistinguished and rather wasted years at Cambridge, Darwin had a five-year voyage in HMS *Beagle*. On his return he married and settled in Kent where during 1837–44 he formulated his theory of evolution. Atomic theory: the scientific atomic theory (as opposed to speculation) is due to John Dalton, Manchester in 1803.

DNA: the discovery was shared between Cambridge and King's College, London. Theory of gravity: the famous apple tree was in the garden of Woolsthorpe Manor, near Grantham, where Newton spent the plague years 1665–7.

Norman Thorpe, Whalley, Lancs

I heard recently that in the 1930s there was a property in Bolton called Sod Hall, which my grandfather wanted to buy. Did it, or does it, exist?

Sod Hall was a property off Clegg's Lane, Little Hulton, an old district still referred to as 'near Bolton, Lancs'. It is shown on the Ordnance Survey map, published 1 November 1950. The hall is not mentioned in local guidebooks published by the Old Little Hulton UDC, though many local people recall that a Victorian or earlier building was there until a few years after the Second World War. This was called Sod Hall Farm and was occupied by several generations of the Shaw family. The farm was bulldozed in about 1960 to make way for new housing. The old name was revived by a tradesman who opened the Sod Hall Mini-Market and General Store almost opposite the original site, but the store closed a few years ago.

B. Rogerson, Swinton, Manchester

I can't help the questioner, but on the Kent approaches to the Dartford Tunnel there is a house proudly called 'Llamedos'. I conclude that the owner is not Welsh but merely has an inverted sense of humour.

Peter Bourne, Ketton, Lincs

On the same lines, there is an ex-police house, now in private ownership, in the village of Hollesley, near the Suffolk coast. Its name these days is Evening Hall.

David Mackness, Ipswich

In the village Wisbech St Mary's in Cambridgeshire, there is a fancy house built a few years ago by a local entrepreneur with a reputation for doing regular battle with the authorities (particularly the planning department). The house is called Fockham Hall.

John Webb, New Romney, Kent

Where and when was the first one-way street introduced in Britain?

During the first ten or twenty years of the nineteenth century, Italian opera was so popular at the King's Theatre in London, and the Haymarket so crowded that 'the nobility were asked to give directions to their servants to set down and take up at the theatre with their horses' heads turned towards Pall Mall'.

John Cooper, Cheam, Surrey

In an article on the Froncysyllte aqueduct, the *Guardian* quoted Telford as stipulating no more than three narrowboats to be on it at one time. Why? Surely the number of boats does not make any difference to the weight on the piers?

Archimedes' rules are OK for barges if there is no motion. The problem arises when they are moving – particularly if an over-zealous bargee speeds up behind a second slower-moving barge. A wave of water may then be trapped between the two barges that is deeper than the previous equilibrium depth. Hence a barge race could lead to overloading. This is probably what Telford had in mind.

John Hallett, Reno, Nevada, US

The questioner is correct. A barge floats due to the Principle of Archimedes. That is to say, the volume of water displaced by the vessel weighs the same as the barge and its contents. Consequently, everything is in equilibrium.

Incidentally, when the aqueduct was opened on 26 November 1805, six boats crossed the structure in a procession. The engineers were in the fourth one, suggesting they had a fair degree of confidence in their aqueduct.

Philip Parker, senior project engineer,
British Waterways, Northwich, Cheshire

I expect they had in mind the weight of the draught-horses on the towpath!

T. Bolton, Orrell, Lancs

The questioner should stop thinking about pier pressure. If the aqueduct contains more than three boats there will not be enough water left in the trough to allow them to progress efficiently. Taken to an extreme, if the aqueduct had narrow boats nose to tail along its length, there would be an almost total displacement of water.

R. A. Stewart, Hanwell, London W7

R. A. Stewart is surely wrong when he says that 'if the aqueduct had narrow boats nose to tail along its length, there would be an almost total displacement of water.'

The displacement of water would indeed be equal to the combined weight of the boats, but it would be spread along the total length of the canal, making no significant difference to the depth of water on the aqueduct.

Harry Rushton, Cheshire

Boats would increase the weight on the piers if the aqueduct were sealed tight by lock gates at each end, and the boats lowered into the water from a crane; then all the displaced water would stay in the channel and the weight on the piers would increase. This doesn't happen normally when a boat enters the aqueduct as the displaced water flows out into the canal at either end. If we could compute the total pressure exerted on the bed of the whole length of the canal, we would find that any extra boat in the water adds to the pressure briefly until the displaced water flows out of the nearest overflow – or indefinitely if the water level is lower than the maximum. The aqueduct, being a part of that canal bed, must take a share of that extra pressure, however small and insignificant in practice.

David Nelson, Dunfermline, Fife

If Essex, Sussex, Wessex and Middlesex belonged to Saxons in the east, south, west and middle respectively, what happened to the Saxons in the north?

They lived in Nosex, so they all died out.

Malcolm Brown, Glasgow; Peter Mair, The Netherlands;
Helena Corran, Bath; and many more . . .

The questioner is overestimating the importance of the South Saxons. In the historic period after the initial Anglo-Saxon invasions, Sussex was largely ignored as an unimportant backwater. After an initially fierce invasion that led the South Saxon king Aelle to be recognized as overlord of all the English, Sussex seemed to have been rigidly contained within not very extensive boundaries and rapidly sank from sight – the *Anglo-Saxon Chronicle* does not mention Sussex between 491 and 675. By the time Sussex was conquered by Offa of Mercia in the eighth century, the South Saxons were divided up and owing allegiance to at least three local kinglets.

At the time the Anglo-Saxon kingdoms were being formed in the middle of the sixth century, the Saxons were basically divided into the West Saxons and the East Saxons. At some earlier point there had been a people occupying the land to the west of London who, from their position between the West and East Saxons, were known as Middle Saxons. But, by the late sixth century, Middlesex north of the Thames had been absorbed with London into Essex, while Middlesex south of the Thames (southern district, Surrey) was disputed between Wessex and Kent.

The 'middle' in Middlesex therefore refers to midway between east and west. In any case, the Angles of Mercia began beyond Watford.

Colin Pilkington, Ormskirk, Lancs

Two upland meadows near Ribblehead in the Yorkshire Dales are called 'Woofa'. Woof is a local surname too. What's the origin?

The name is almost certainly a form of 'wolf', used perhaps as a name for someone with the character of a wolf or as a placename for somewhere frequented by wolves. Near Scarborough is a Woof Howe, spelt Woulfhow in some early documents. Woofa Bank is a field name near Burley. And what about Wolverhampton and the many Wolvertons?

John Bishop, Kirkby Malzeard, North Yorks

I wish to correct John Bishop on the derivation of 'Wolverhampton'. The town's name has no connection with Wolves. It comes from the Saxon Wolfrunas Hean Tun, meaning 'the high town under the patronage of the Lady Wulfruna', who gave the town its charter in the tenth century.

J. Foote, Wolverhampton

Does anyone know the origin of the phrase 'The One-Eyed City' used by Liverpudlians to describe Birkenhead, the town on the opposite bank of the Mersey?

Birkenhead is a shipbuilding town and the low job in the yard was that of a catcher who caught the red-hot end of rivets in a brass bowl as the ship was built. Hence Birkenhead became a town of many one-eyed men.

Don Webb, London SW6

This is because there is one 'i' in Birkenhead. If Don Webb's answer related to shipbuilding were correct, then Belfast, Glasgow and Newcastle would also be referred to as one 'i' cities, but of course they are not because they don't have an 'i'.

Les Jones, Birkenhead, Merseyside

I was born in Birkenhead and was brought up in neighbouring Wallasey. My mother used to tell me that the name arose because there were so many unsolved crimes there – people in Birkenhead used to go round with one eye closed (metaphorically, I presume) and so never noticed crimes taking place!

Joan Machell, Lancaster

Neither Salford, Gateshead, Birkenhead nor any other place can lay exclusive claim to being the one-eyed city. The *OED* gives 'one-eyed' as: 'a general term of disapproval or contempt: small, inferior, inadequate, unimportant, esp. of a town'. It quotes an 1871 usage by D. G. Rossetti: 'Lechlade . . . being but a "one-eyed town"

as the Yankees say'; and other places, including Tobago.
The epithet often seemed to be given to a place situated
in the shadow of a more important one, e.g. Manchester,
Newcastle or Liverpool.

Fritz Spiegl, Liverpool

At one time the town of Birkenhead was still so small in
comparison to Liverpool that an observer on the Liverpool
bank of the Mersey was able to encompass in field of
view the full width of Birkenhead with one eye closed;
hence the somewhat derisory phrase.

Jim Doyle, Liverpool

Where is the longest continuous downhill road in Britain that can legally be used by a cyclist?

The *Contour Road Book of Scotland*, produced by Harry
Inglis in 1900, shows dramatic diagrams for cyclists of
the ups and downs on all the major roads of Scotland.
The highest and steepest is over twelve miles from
Tornapress to Applecross, from sea level to 2,000 ft and
back to sea level. For longer but more gentle descents
there are several stretches of about ten miles, such as 600
ft from near Elvanfoot to Beattock, or 1,100 ft from the
Devil's Elbow to Braemar. Further books were produced
for England and Wales, and the eleven miles from Pen-y-

pass to Betws-y-coed is mainly downhill but has some small undulations on the way. The steepest roads in the books are at Lynmouth and Porlock.

Gavin Ross, Harpenden, Herts

Gavin Ross points out various contenders in Scotland and Wales. Those wishing to consider off-road variants would do well to include the Roman road 'High Street' in the Lake District. From the summit of High Raise the 'road' descends to Penrith – about eleven miles away. Heading south from High Raise gives you an almost unbroken descent in Troutbeck and Windermere, again in the region of eleven miles. Unfortunately, either way you have to cycle eleven miles continuously uphill to get to the start point.

Matthew Holmes, Leamington Spa, Warks

Why are so many country roads called Pound Lane?

Because the countryside tends to be anti-Euro.

Graham Guest, London SE19

Having recently spent some time using the backroads of Britain, I can only assume they are so called because that is the average amount of money spent on maintaining them.

David Donnell, London SW14

There is a country road near Cambridge, between Cottenham and Wilburton, called Twenty Pence Road. Pound Lane is obviously just a case of inflation.

Michael Grosvenor Myer, Cambridge

They are simply named after the pound that once stood in them. The pound would have been (at least in later years) a stone building, sometimes roofed, with a secure door or gate. It was an important element in the rural infra-structure. In it were impounded stray livestock found trespassing in the area. Each manor or parish would employ a hayward (hedge warden), beadle or pinder whose responsibility was to protect growing crops from damage and consumption by wandering cattle, horses and the like. The beasts' release to their owners would have been dependent upon payment to the pound-keeper of sums to cover their keep, plus a pledge of compensation to the victim of the trespass.

John Kruse, London WC1

The term is not universal. The Kirklees Metropolitan area of West Yorkshire includes not a single Pound Lane, but no less than six Pinfold Lanes, all in different parishes. In this part of the country a pinfold is, of course, an enclo-sure for stray animals.

Mike Swift, Birchencliffe, Huddersfield

There are also many Pound Streets (e.g. Wendover, Bucks) and Pound Cottages (e.g. Wheatley, Oxon). And Pound Acre, Pound Close, Pound Piece, Pound Pightle, etc., can be found in John Field's *English Field Names* (Sutton, 1989).

John Vince, Aylesbury, Bucks

Visitors to the Stone Inn in Kings Norton, Birmingham, can 'buy beer by the pound', the pub being adjacent to the village pound.

Duncan Cameron, Thornton, Lancs

It's not just in the country that Pound Lanes are found. Willesden, north London, has a Pound Lane. It also has a Euro Close, though there are no clues in the vicinity as to just how close.

Alex Foord, Willesden, London

Duncan Cameron is correct in all respects save two. The Stone Inn is in Northfield, not Kings Norton, across the road from the ancient parish church. The saying should be: 'You can buy a pint by the stone or by the pound', thus preserving three traditional imperial measurements.

Paddy Powell, Banstead, Surrey

Which sea is the 'Alley Alley Oh' and was there a real big ship that sank 'on the last day of September'?

I first heard the ditty 'The big ship sails down the ally, alley, oh/On the last day of December' on a visit to Manchester in the late 1920s. It was popularly sung by children as an accompaniment to their skipping. The foundation of the words was from the Manchester Ship Canal, which was built to allow seagoing vessels to sail into the industrial heart of the city, mainly for the benefit of the textile business. That was the 'alley, ally oh'.

The canal was officially opened on 1 January 1894, hence the first ship sailed up the alley on 31 December 1893 to be in position for the grand opening.

Rowland O'Rostron, Enniskean, Cork, Ireland

I am not convinced by Rowland O'Rostron's explanation that the 'Alley Alley Oh' is the Manchester Ship Canal. The first recorded complete voyage along the full length of the Ship Canal was on 7 December 1893 by the Board of Directors of the Ship Canal Company aboard the SS *Snowdrop*. The opening to traffic was marked by procession of vessels on 1 January 1894. The first vessel in the procession was the yacht *Norseman*, while the first vessel to unload a commercial cargo was the SS *Fraternity* belonging to the CWS. There is no record of a voyage on the 'last day of December' and certainly no ship was sunk on this occasion. The official opening was not until 21 May 1894, when Queen Victoria travelled the length of the terminal docks aboard the Admiralty yacht *Enchantress*.

Frank Shackleton, Rochdale

The not so good ships that sank on the 'Alley Alley Oh' were the coffin ships that went down in the Atlantic Ocean, all too often in the annual November tempests, before the advent of the Plimsoll line legislation.

Roy Hollingworth, Horsforth, Leeds

In *The Singing Game* (Oxford, 1985), Iona and Peter Opie point out that the song could not have been composed to celebrate the opening of the Manchester Ship Canal: 'this seems to be precluded by a recollection of the [song] in New Zealand in 1870' (Brian Sutton-Smith, in *The Games of New Zealand Children* (1959), cites 'The Eely Ily Oh' at Nelson, NZ, *c.* 1870). The Opies add that, although it is improbable that the line evolved from the nautical order 'Lee-oh', songs of the sea include the cries 'a lee, a lee-oh' or 'ee-lee-ay-lee-oh'. Also, the day in the last line varies from the 'last day in December' (Swanage as well as Shelagh Delaney's Salford) to that in September (Birmingham), or even 'the 14th of November' or 'Christmas Day in the morning'.

Frank McManus, Tordmorden, Lancs

Tourists-who-prefer-to-think-of-themselves-as-travellers often seem obsessed with finding the real France, the real India, etc. Where could travellers find the real Britain, or the real London? Where do the rest of us live?

The real Britain is to be found in the village of Ashton under Hill between Tewkesbury and Evesham, where the customers in the public house speak with real Ambridge accents. The real London is found in its taxis (monoglot); buses and underground (polyglot); and suburban trains (no speech there, because 'London reserve' prevails).

John Wymer, Bridport, Dorset

Anywhere a coach party can't get to.

Matthew Guite, Staines, Middx

Britain's film industry is in Holland, its press in Australia, its manufacturing in Asia, its financial policies are set in Germany, its military command is in the District of Columbia, and the Beefeaters are in the Tower.

Art Hilgart, Kalamazoo, Michigan, US

The thousands of tourists who visit Brighton each year see pretty much the same bits that I see, with the exception of my flat and the office where I work. In my opinion, the 'real' Britain (or India or France) is not a geographical location, it is the society in which we live. Thus, in order to really experience a country, it is essential to speak the language and live in the community. However, if one does the latter, one is no longer a traveller. I would therefore suggest that there is no difference between 'tourist' and 'traveller'.

Veronica Tapp, Brighton

Why 'Blighty'? Does this term refer to the UK, Great Britain or England only?

Like much British Army slang, Blighty is of Indian origin. It comes from Hindi and Urdu *vilayat*, meaning foreign (particularly Western) parts. *Vilayat* was itself borrowed from Arabic, via Persian: it originally meant 'province', and was used in particular of Afghanistan when it was a province of the Mughal Empire (R. S. McGregor, *The Oxford Hindi-English Dictionary*). During the Raj it naturally came to be used of the place from which the foreign soldiers came, which is how the soldiers themselves picked it up. *Vilayati*, 'of vilayat' (pronounced with the main stress on the 'la' and a secondary one on the 'ti'), easily turned into 'Blighty'. It gained wide currency during the World War, when a 'Blighty one' was a wound serious enough for the soldier to be sent back to Britain. The word would then have been applied to any part of the

UK, then still including Ireland. In modern Hindi, *vilayat* is used in a more general way of Britain, Europe or the West.

Valerie Roebuck, Whalley Range, Manchester

'Welcome' signs on county borders, which logic would suggest should be back-to-back, are rarely so. And the signs on the M6 at the Scottish/English border are about half a mile apart. Who administers these strips of no-man's land between counties?

Welcome signs are not necessarily erected precisely on the boundaries: they are for the general information of travellers rather than for the demarcation of land ownership and municipal responsibility. They are usually sited to be convenient and easy-to-read for motorists, rather than back-to-back on the actual boundary – which would often, for example, be on the very middle of a river bridge. Local councils are increasingly using such boundary signs also for publicity purposes, such as 'Norwich – a fine city', for which an eye-catching site is important. A more accurate indication of exact county boundaries is an obvious change in the road surfaces marking the end and the beginning of maintenance responsibility.

Michael Smith, Swaffham, Norfolk

The welcome sign at the point where the Glasgow to Carlisle railway line crosses the Scottish/English border states: 'Welcome to England – Haste ye back'.

Philip Reeves, Glasgow

Did Shrop, Wilt and Hamp once exist as county towns?

They are Shrewsbury, Wilton and Southampton. The county names are phonetic renderings of names in which some syllables have been elided or omitted altogether. When the *Anglo-Saxon Chronicle* was being written, Shropshire was spelt Scrobbesbyrigscir, Wiltshire was Wiltunscir and Hampshire was Hamtunscir, each meaning 'the shire with Shrewsbury/Wilton/[South]Hampton as its chief town'.

The process of elision began very early: the *Anglo-Saxon Chronicle* later records Shropshire as Scrobscyr, and the *Domesday Book* records Hampshire as Hantescire. This process is still happening: we pronounce Gloucester as Gloster, and Brighton, until recently, was spelt Brighthelmstone.

Southampton was, in early Saxon times, the major town of Hampshire, whence the county's name. It only lost that status when Winchester became the royal capital, but retained its pre-eminence within the county when the court and government moved to London. Hampshire was still known formally as The County of Southampton as late as 1959.

Bruce Purvis, Salisbury Library, Wiltshire

'Bungerly Hippingstone' in Lancashire was the site of Henry VI's capture prior to his imprisonment in the Tower of London. What kind of place was it, and what is the origin of the name?

Henry VI was captured at Brungerley Hipping Stones, near Clitheroe. The Hipping Stones were stepping stones across the River Ribble, close to the place where the river was forded by the Clitheroe–Waddington Road. The present day Brungerley Bridge is close to the spot.

David Johns, Supervisor, Clitheroe Information Centre

If Northern Ireland is a province and Wales is a principality, what is Scotland?

Scotland is a kingdom. In 1603, James VI, who was already King of Scotland, became also James I, King of England. Although both Scotland and England remained kingdoms, during the seventeenth century the habit of referring to the 'United Kingdoms' developed. Even late in the eighteenth century, people were writing letters to the press about 'the defence of these united kingdoms'. The use of 'United Kingdom' (singular) is relatively modern. Furthermore, if Scotland returns to independence, the United Kingdom will cease to exist. The Province and the Principality don't count; the legal and historical definition of the United Kingdom is that it is the Union of the Kingdoms of Scotland and England.

Dave Coull, Dundee

Northern Ireland isn't a province, it is part (six counties) of the (nine-county) Province of Ulster. The other three counties are in the Republic.

Tim McBride, Kingston-upon Thames, Surrey

While Dave Coull is correct to say that James VI, King of Scots, became King of England, he should know that, historically, only the Scottish people are the sovereigns of Scotland. Her Majesty, Queen Elizabeth II of England, is rightfully Her Grace, Queen of Scots and, indeed, will continue to be so in the event of Scottish independence.

Norman Stewart, Wark, Northumberland

The *Times Atlas of the World* describes Wales as a constituent principality of the United Kingdom, Northern Ireland as a constituent region and Scotland as a constituent country. That the questioner does not ask about

England suggests that he has an erroneous view of the United Kingdom. England is a constituent country, just like Scotland.

Harry Bovis, London NW5

PLACES OVERSEAS

If Napoleon had won the battle of Waterloo, would things have been so bad?

Arguably, it would only have led to a lengthening of the Napoleonic wars. According to Elizabeth Longford in her biography of Wellington, he commented to one of his generals before the battle that he had picked the site out a year earlier and 'tucked it in my pocket'. This was because of the reverse slope (now destroyed to make the mound for the Belgian memorial to the battle) and also because the woods behind the Allies' position were free from undergrowth. Thus, if defeated, Wellington's army (or at least the more disciplined parts of it) could have retreated in good order through it, living to fight another day if neither night nor Blucher had intervened in time.

Brian Goldfarb, Leicester

Never mind what would have happened if we had lost the battle of Waterloo – Agincourt was the real lost opportunity. If the Welsh archers had shot the other way, they could have finished off the English aristocracy and spared us 600 years of English cooking.

Roger Backhouse, Ilford, Essex

I would find myself living somewhere else, as we don't seem to name places after defeats.

Bob Waring, Waterloo, Merseyside

No, we would have had a republic, been members of the euro and had a decent legal system, rather than one made up by geriatric judges as they muddle along.

John Pilsbury, Wrexham

They would have been worse; we'd be drinking beer in litres.

Ray Banks, Doncaster

Not for England, which ruled the seas; but it would not have been so good for Belgium, whose present shape might have remained on the drawing board. In place of the Congress of Vienna there would have been a standoff. Prussia would have retired to north Germany and become more introspective. Perhaps a move to unite the German states would have happened without them, leaving a placid southern Germanic 'empire' under Bavaria's rule. The Franco–Prussian war might never have happened.

As for France, the overtaxed and over-recruited populace would surely have evicted Napoleon soon after Waterloo, leaving the ambitious Marshall Soult to run an interim administration – one with which all but England could have reached an understanding.

French nationalism would have brought back Napoleon's heir sooner, allowing France to establish a greater European hegemony by default. The First World War would have been transformed into an Austro–Russian affair, with England and France acting as arbiters. Otherwise, not much difference.

Malcolm Sweetman, Aldeburgh, Suffolk

Non.

Jacques LeBlanc, London E11

It would have been a pity as we would not have had the story of Woodrow Wyatt spelling out his name to a receptionist at a French hotel thus: Waterloo, Ypres, Agincourt, Trafalgar, Trafalgar.

Patrick Brittain, London

Bob Waring, of Waterloo in Merseyside, suggests we don't name places after defeats, but he could move to Nottingham and take up residence in Isandula

(Isandhlwana) Road. The massacre at Isandula was not one of our better results against the Zulu Impis. In the same area of late Victorian housing we have Zulu Road, Chard Street, Durnford Street, Chelmsford Street, Pearson Street and Eland Road. Chard was in charge of the defence of Rorke's Drift, Durnford led the relief column, Chelmsford was a senior officer, Pearson one of his officers, and the Eland is a local river.

Keith Sherratt, Nottingham

Have American soldiers ever faced Russian soldiers in combat, officially or unofficially, and if so, who won?

US forces fought in Russia during 1918–19. They were part of an Allied force from Britain, Australia and France that was sent to secure Russia first from the Germans and then from the Bolsheviks. The US troops, known as the Polar Bears, served in northern Russia under British command. Around 600 troops provided medical and logististical services as well as frontline troops. During this time, the Polar Bears did engage with Russian soldiers and the outcome was not a favourable one – US troops pulled out and were replaced by the British and French.

Keith Bedson, Hornsea, East Yorks

In his book *America's Siberian Adventure*, published in 1931, Major General William Graves describes how he was ordered to undertake a secret mission under direct orders of the US secretary of war Newton D. Baker. He travelled to Vladivostok, taking command of US forces consisting of two infantry regiments and auxiliary units – 12,500 men in all – whose task was to protect Allied military stores in depots along the trans-Siberian railway, to aid the Czechoslovak Legion stranded in Siberia, and to discourage Japanese plans to annex Russian territories during the civil war that followed the Russian Revolution. The trans-Siberian railway was then mostly being used for military supplies in support of the Allied attempt to prevent the spread of Bolshevism.

Interestingly, the American forces suffered more attacks and problems from the White Army than from the Red Army.

The US troops had a few clashes, notably when the Cossack ataman Semenoff decided to wipe out a boxcar full of American soldiers in order to be able to accuse the Bolsheviks and thus bring the US in against them (this failed).

In the end, the American troops were brought home without any fanfare, and the adventure was deemed one of the most ill-conceived interventions in American history up to that time. Graves, who led the expedition, was accused of being a 'Red sympathizer' and was generally disgraced after the event.

Nader Fekri, Hebden Bridge, Yorks

Only relatively recently did it become known that many of the Chinese and Korean fighter aircraft involved in the Korean war of 1950–53 were in fact flown by Russian pilots, introduced secretly by the Soviet Union to bolster the communist forces of the North against their American opponents.

Ordered to dress in Chinese uniforms and speak Korean over the radio, many of these Soviet pilots were veterans of the Second World War and were much more effective than their North Korean counterparts, who were poorly trained and inexperienced. The principal aircraft involved were the Russian MiG-15 and the US F-86 Sabre, both first-generation jets. Comparisons of aircraft capability are notoriously difficult; as is often the case, each had advantages and disadvantages, making the skills of the pilot the deciding factor on most occasions.

Ultimately, however, insufficient Russian pilots were committed to make a real difference; by the end of hostilities, a kill-to-loss ratio of around 10:1 in favour of the US is generally accepted. Pilots from both sides reached 'ace' status, however, and in the late nineties met officially for the first time as part of a scheme to help resolve cases of airmen missing in action.

Chris Rogers, Edgware, Middx

Is it true that during the Second World War, the

Irish embassy in Berlin was staffed right up until the arrival of the Russian army? If so, what were they doing there?

The Irish legation (not embassy) had left Berlin before the arrival of the Russians. The original legation building had been destroyed in an RAF incendiary raid in November 1943, and it was moved to a stud farm at Staffelde outside Berlin.

Ireland's strict (official) neutrality meant that diplomatic relations were maintained with the Axis, as well as Allied governments, throughout the war. Germany, Italy and Japan all maintained legations in Dublin in this period.

The Irish legation staff were responsible for the small number of Irish citizens living in Reich territories, they argued the Irish position in relation to neutrality and they made complaints and claims for reparations for the several incidences of Luftwaffe bombings of Ireland. In addition, the legation reported back to Dublin on issues including Nazi propaganda efforts aimed at the republic.

There has also been speculation about the wartime role of the legation in supplying Irish passports and other documentation to individuals not entitled to them, although there are several recorded incidences of the legation refusing such requests, rightly suspecting that the documents were to be used to slip German spies into Eire.

Stephen Ryan, Harold's Cross, Dublin

The Eire government in the Second World War wasn't strictly neutral. A flax and linen factory was operated in Co Donegal funded by the British government and webbing was made for parachute straps for the British army. In Dublin the British authorities ran an employment office that recruited Irish nationals for transport, mining jobs etc. in England and the maintenance of this infrastructure allowed more to go into the war effort.

Flying boats stationed in Co Fermanagh, Northern Ireland, were permitted to use an air corridor across the republic, as it came to be known, so that they could go on patrol in the north Atlantic more quickly and use less fuel. Also, any British fighting personnel who fetched up in Ireland were immediately repatriated while Germans were interned until the end of the war.

This all excludes the huge contribution by Irish both South and North (where conscription was not brought in) who joined the British military forces.

Patrick Brogan, Omagh, Northern Ireland

Is there a planet anywhere in the universe that the rest of the world can go to now George Bush is re-elected?

I would suggest that it is easier and more cost efficient to send Mr Bush and his administration off to another place where he can continue making the world a 'safer' place. I think the seventh planet of our solar system would be appropriate.

Joyce Rankin, Co Antrim, Northern Ireland

Why do Americans have math and sports, while you Brits have maths and sport?

This is obvious. 'Maths' because it's an abbreviation of a plural, similar to ops for operations. Off the top of my head I can't think of another common example of a plural abbreviated to a singular, whether in American or English, so 'math' makes no logical sense. However, given that Americans have been mistakenly referring to 'aluminum' since 1812 or so, there is little prospect of reversal.

'Sport' because it's a generic description of activity undertaken in pursuit of a wide variety of sports.

The American language seems to develop with little regard for logic anyway: my favourite is the increasing use of the hybrid 'irregardless' (from regardless and irrespective, presumably), which, like 'I could care less', means exactly the opposite of what one would otherwise infer.

Richard Savory, Witney, Oxon

Richard Savory would not regard the Americanism 'I could care less' as illogical were he to add the question mark which should be at the end.

I am reminded of the Russian Jewish dissident in the 1930s whose exile from his home town was only lifted when he signed a letter to the mayor stating: 'Stalin was right. I was wrong. I should apologize.' His friends were aghast at his apparent denial of his refusenik principles until he pointed out that the letter had omitted the question mark at the end of each sentence.

This, I believe, is rhetorical irony.

Andy Bebington, Croydon

Do the Inuit cook? If so, how do they get a fire started and what do they burn?

Fire was made by the Inuit by simply striking together iron and pyrites over dry moss. In summer they would have cooked outside over an open fire. However, I suspect Peter Hanson inquires about the method of cooking in an igloo. Light and heat were provided by a large stone lamp (*qudlirn*); this was a basin filled with whale or seal blubber with a moss wick. Over this was hung a stone kettle (*ukusik*). Most food was simply boiled in this, though much was also eaten raw. Tasty . . .

John Kruse, London E17

Yes. They start a fire the same way you or I do: with a match, which burns wood; a lighter, which burns petroleum, or the stove, which burns grease and maybe dinner.

Emily Greenberg, Douglas, Isle of Man

According to folklore, many years ago two Inuit fishermen tried to cook their favourite meal while in their boat and perished in the ensuing fire. Hence the well-known expression: you can't have your kayak and heat it.

Terry Mahoney, Bury St Edmunds

One of the most fascinating questions in Notes & Queries asked, when a decision was made in Rome at the height of the Roman Empire, how long it took the news to reach Hadrian's Wall, and how it got there? There hasn't been a single response. Does that mean no one knows?

I know.

John Gray, York

So, no Roman archaeologists have answered. Perhaps the question has yet to reach them.

Ian Ground, Newcastle upon Tyne

Strictly speaking, yes: we have no direct evidence on this subject. One might produce an estimate of a 'typical' journey time on the basis of evidence for the speed of different sorts of transport in the Roman Empire; there is also the evidence from Egypt of the time-lag between the death of an emperor and the last mention of him, or the first mention of his successor, in official documents – sometimes as long as three or four months. At best, one could hope for a plausible estimate of the typical journey time, bearing in mind that this would change significantly according to the season, and that unexpected delays of weeks or even months were commonplace.

Neville Morley, Department of Classics
& Ancient History, University of Bristol

This question assumes that the centre of government, in the person of the emperor, was always in Rome. In fact emperors moved about, basing themselves in various locations where their presence would be most effective, including Milan, Trier, the Danube frontier and provincial capitals of the eastern empire. Several emperors lived for a time in York, including Hadrian himself, Septimius Severus, Constantius Chlorus and Constantine the Great, in which case messages to military commanders on the wall could probably be delivered within a day.

Michael Short, Rye, East Sussex

How long a message would take to get somewhere in the Roman empire would naturally depend in part on how important the message was and how determined the messengers were. According to Plutarch, the news of Nero's death was brought to his successor, Galba, at Clunia in Spain seven days later.

Clunia was a good 1,100 miles from Rome by road, giving a speed of more than 150 miles a day. The messenger may in this case have travelled partly by sea, but similar speeds in emergencies are recorded for purely land journeys. However, under the more normal official system, imperial messengers travelled in light carriages and averaged less than 50 miles a day.

A similar journey north from Rome to Hadrian's Wall was around 1,500 miles, including a sea-crossing. If the message were a vital one delivered at maximum speed, it could theoretically have been there in as little as ten to eleven days, but normally it would have taken more than a month.

David Levene, professor of Latin language and literature,
School of Classics, University of Leeds

On the reverse of the Chinese one yuan note there is an image of the Great Wall of China. Underneath are three scripts, one of which appears to be Arabic. Is it Arabic? And what is it doing there?

Well spotted. I see this after looking carefully too, and after a bit of Googling, it appears it is Arabic of some kind. Apparently it means 'Great Horde' and was issued by Kublai Khan. Don't forget Kublai Khan, grandson of Genghis Khan, was from Mongolia, which is part of today's China. And Chinese notes all seem to depict every possible ethnic background – just look at the range of their currency and the inscriptions, symbols and pictures on them.

Tushar Walhekar, Maidenhead

No, it isn't Arabic, but Uighur, a Turkic language that happens to be written in a modification of the Arabic alphabet. The other languages in the banknote are Zhuang, Mongolian and Tibetan, i.e. the languages of the (formally) Autonomous Provinces of China.

Paulo Rocha, Braga, Portugal

What is the longest football team name in the world?

The longest name in the English league is my team, Brighton and Hove Albion, with twenty-one letters. However, Borussia Mönchengladbach, of the Bundesliga is twenty-three letters long. There must be longer names in Germany, though.

Tony Greenfield, Brighton

Some contenders would be: Amsterdamsche Football Club Ajax (Holland, 29); Real Sociedad de San Sebastian (Spain, 26); Zalaegerszegi Torna Egylet (Hungary, 24); Football Club Rotor Volgograd (Russia, 26); Internazionale de Milano (Italy, 22) and Genclerbirligi Ankara spor Klubu (Turkey, 29).

Ian Ogier, Guernsey

Bournemouth and Boscombe Athletic has 30.

Mark Power, Dublin

IIIINNNGGG-UUUUURRRR-LAAAAAAANNND-DDDD has 35 . . . and 38 in some versions of the chant.

Dominic Rice, Brussels, Belgium

Dynamo Llanfairpwllgwyngyllgogerychwyrndrobwyllllantysiliogogogoch FC.

Pete, Cambridge

The former side Horwich Railway Mechanics Institute Football Club would have been a contender. However, with a move to a neighbouring town, it has been shortened to Leigh Railway Mechanics Institute Football Club.

Aidan Corcoran, Bolton

Ballvereinborussiadortmundneunzehnhundertundneun

(BVB09 Dortmund Germany) and probably another dozen German teams.

Kevin Elliott, Berlin

Tetaumatawhakatangihangakoauaotamateaurehaeaturipuk-apihimaungahoronukupokaiwhenuaakitanarahu is a place in New Zealand. Wonder if they have a football team?

Tom, Hosham, Surrey

Most people in this country are against blood sports and hunting animals. Do they have the same anti-blood sports lobby against bullfighting in Spain and other places where the practice takes place?

There is certainly an anti-bullfighting lobby in Spain. It is not as vociferous as the anti-hunt lobby – they don't make protests at bullfights (probably for personal safety reasons), but in Seville there are frequent appearances of 'Toros no!' graffiti on statues and buildings.

Richard Avery, Alcalá de Guadaíra, Spain

I don't know about Spain, but bullfighting is a very pop-ular tradition in Mexico and is unquestioningly accepted. It has a certain cachet to it, with old-world, landed-gentry associations, and bullfights in Mexico City are basically an opportunity to be photographed in a posh gown if you're a local soap diva, or with a soap diva hanging off your arm if you're a wealthy businessman. People have absolutely no notion that this 'sport' can even be considered offensive (even the most progressive Mexican TV channel, Canal Once, dedicates a weekly, half-hour show to it). Mexicans tend to just look at me like I'm a bit weird and humour me when I start going on about animal rights and cheering when the bullfighter gets gored.

Alistair McCreadie, Mexico City

When and where did the notion of diplomatic immunity come about? Is this enforceable by international law and how far does it extend e.g. in the case of a murder inquiry?

Diplomatic immunity is an essential underpinning of the business of diplomacy itself – how else could our representatives safely serve in a hostile country? It is enshrined in, I think, the Vienna Convention (I suspect a series of conventions). It only covers people who stick to diplomatic immunity as defined (and hence spies using diplomatic cover can, if discovered, be expelled) but in principle it covers everything they do. (Remember that back in the eighties the police were not allowed into the

Libyan embassy to identify and/or detain the killer of PC Yvonne Fletcher.) It can, however, be waived by the diplomat's own country, and that is sometimes done in the interests of good relations.

Keith Long, Kingston upon Thames, Surrey

The idea of diplomatic immunity dates back to Ancient Greece. Special status was given to foreign envoys visiting the Greek state. Even now, diplomatic immunity does not confer immunity from all laws; rather it means that representatives of foreign governments operate under the laws of their own country while abroad. In practice this does not mean that all diplomats can get away with what they like. In serious cases, they are still likely to be tried under their own laws and at the very least they will be in for a good ticking-off from their bosses.

Max Wurr, Stanmore, Middx

One could also point to the cities of refuge mentioned in the Old Testament. Further, extraterritoriality (of a sort) was recognized by the medieval church. Remember Quasimodo shouting 'Sanctuary'?

Robert del Valle, Detroit, US

What time is it at the North – or indeed South – Pole?

Whatever time you like. As the poles cover all twenty-four time zones, I think the time is usually kept the same as their home base, i.e. Mawson base is Sydney time, the US base at the South Pole is probably New York/Washington time, the French bases are probably Paris time.

Christopher Woods, Mt Victoria, NSW, Australia

In the absence of a time zone, the time at the prime meridian should be applied. Hence the time at the poles should be Greenwich Mean Time.

Vinod Moonesinghe, Rajagiriya, Sri Lanka

Time is an illusion (lunchtime doubly so). The time is not really a problem – if it is not in the total dark time in the winter, you would use solar time. When the sun reaches its maximum height, then it is midday (set your watch accordingly). It is the date that is the problem as the international dateline and meridian merge. I assume there must be an international convention to avoid two polar explorers arriving at a pole at same time on the same day twenty-four hours apart!

G. Baker, South Ockenden, Essex

G. Baker's solution won't work: at the poles the sun rises above the horizon in spring, keeps rising until mid-summer, then starts setting.

Phil Barker, Edinburgh

When we have two hot days in the UK the rail system is thrown into chaos. How do they manage to keep the trains running in countries where it is hot for most of the year?

In Sydney, Australia, the railway lines are constructed to allow normal running of trains up to 38 °C. If the temperature exceeds 38 °C (which on average happens only a few times a year in Sydney), speed restrictions are imposed. Presumably it wasn't considered necessary for railways in Britain to be able to withstand such temperatures, so they weren't constructed to be able to do so.

Simon Arjankeizer, Sydney, Australia

The problem is not the heat on its own, but the extremes of hot and cold. The metal rails expand in the heat and contract in the cold. They used to be laid in short sections bolted together. Each join had enough room for the rail to expand without buckling. The rails are now laid in much longer sections and are welded together, which makes them harder wearing and gives a smoother ride. The downside is that there's no room for expansion. To get around this, they are put under tension when they are laid – more tension means they can withstand a higher temperature. However, they would then buckle in the cold as the rails contract. Since we have cold winters, there needs to be a trade-off between being able to withstand both heat and cold. To be fair to the rail companies, we very rarely have more than 30 °C heat, so the rails aren't designed to withstand it.

Rick Webber, Brighton

It's to do with thermal expansion coefficients I think. For instance, a 10 metre piece of steel at 15 °C will be 2 mm longer at 30 °C. It is easy to see why over longer stretches of rail this can lead to buckling.

Patrick Brown, London

Do countries other than Britain have equivalents of John O'Groats and Land's End that are regularly used as start and finish points for charity walks/cycles etc.?

The recognized end-to-end in Ireland is from Malin Head, the most northerly point in County Donegal, to Mizen Head in Cork, the most south-westerly point. The sea area forecast on the radio opens with both placenames.

John Maguire, Dublin

In The Netherlands, there is the 'Pieterpad' ('Pieter Track'), which runs from the northern village of Pieterburen to the St Pieters mountain in the south. Although there are places further north and south respectively, it is a nice idea to walk from one 'Pieter' to the other (although the Pieters have nothing in common). The track is a few hundred kilometres long, roughly along the eastern border of The Netherlands and walking it takes a few days.

Johan van Slooten, Urk, The Netherlands

As I found out on moving to New Zealand, they have a saying 'from Cape Reinga to the Bluff', meaning something nationwide. Cape Reinga is at the top of a peninsula with a small settlement on the most northerly tip of New Zealand's north island. The Bluff refers to the town of Bluff – a small fishing town right at the bottom of the south island. Though, oddly, they ignore the fact that there is another inhabited island further south.

Henry, Colb, New Zealand

At school in the 1940s I was taught that Mount Everest was 29,002 ft high. In a recent Oxford encyclopaedia I see that it is now 29,028 ft (8,848 metres). What has happened to the mountain and/or its measurement over the years?

The original height of Mt Everest, or Peak XV as it was known when first surveyed by the British in India in the mid-1800s, was 29,002 ft. However, this was calculated from 150 miles away in India using theodolites, as Nepal was a closed country. It wasn't until eight years after the initial survey that it was found to be the highest in the world, as there were a great deal of calculations to be made from a great deal of data. Kanchenjunga, which was far more accessible to the British due to its proximity to India, was believed to be the highest.

Once established as the highest and renamed Everest, the height of 29,002 ft was accepted as fact until it was surveyed in the 1950s by the Indians, who gained closer access and had more accurate equipment. They established the height as 29,028 ft, which made the accuracy of the earlier survey more astonishing: a 26 ft inaccuracy from 150 miles away, using Victorian equipment, was quite a feat.

The US conducted a survey in 1999 using GPS receivers placed on the summit and calculated a new height of 29,035 ft (8,850 m). This is the most accurate height to date and is the 'official' height (even though the Natural History Museum still listed Everest as 29,029 ft in 2003).

However, it will have to be revised in the future. The Himalayas are growing at several centimetres a year, because the Indian subcontinent is still pushing into the rest of Asia, and Everest will gain more height.

The Victorian survey did have its ironies. It was initially

started by Sir George Everest – after whom the mountain was named. He was a stickler for accuracy, and the greatest inaccuracy of all is the mispronunciation of Everest. His name was pronounced Eve-Rest, and mispronouncing it as Everest would have irritated him greatly!

John Finch, Plympton, Devon

Mount Everest is 29,002 ft high. I, too, was at school in the 1940s and my geography teacher taught us the same statistic. As everybody who was at school in the forties will know, what Sir told us was true and what all these Johnny-come-lately organizations say is wrong.

Peter S. Barnett, Glossop, Derbyshire

So Mt Everest is 29,035 feet and rising. But why is it so much higher than any other mountain? Have there been higher mountains in the geological past? And are there any theoretical limits to how high a mountain could grow?

David Jarman, Stirling

There is a limit to the height that a mountain can be on earth. This is determined by the pressure exerted on the supporting rock foundation by the weight of the mountain. When the forces exerted on the supporting granite, quartz, silicon dioxide etc., are enough to break the bonds holding the molecules of the supporting material, it liquefies and flows away from the mountain, allowing it to sink.

Robert A. Donald, Edinburgh

My childhood ambition was to climb Everest and scrape two feet off the summit. I couldn't understand why Hillary and Tenzing didn't do it while they were up there.

David Brinicombe, High Bickington, Devon

I heard that, given the conditions and inevitable uncertainty of the original measurements, what the surveyors came up with was an estimate of 'about 29,000 ft'. However, it was felt that if the height was declared to be 29,000 ft, this would be dismissed as either highly unlikely or the rough estimate that it truly was. It was therefore decided to add another two feet to achieve not only a more 'realistic'-looking height but also a spurious degree of accuracy, which is why 29,002 ft went unchallenged until the 1950s.

Quentin Burrell, Ballabeg, Isle of Man

So we know the height of the top of Mt Everest above sea level, but what is sea level? It varies wave by wave, hour by hour, season by season, decade by decade, north by south and east by west. And when we have defined it, how do we measure it? From the top of Mt Everest?

John Widdicombe, London SW20

In answer to John Widdicombe's point, sea level varies considerably according to latitude and there is in fact an equatorial bulge so that at Everest's latitude of approximately 30 °N, sea level is about 16,100 metres higher than it is at the poles, and it is a further 5,300 metres higher at the equator. So, in calculating height according to sea level, the equatorial mountains are at a disadvantage.

In a 1966 article, Isaac Asimov recalculated the heights of mountains to take account of this and created a list of mountain peaks in order of their distance from the centre of the earth. By this standard he estimated that Kilimanjaro would stand 27,200 metres above polar sea level compared with Everest's 25,000, but the overall champion would be the otherwise unheralded Mount Chimborazo in Ecuador, which stands a mere 6,300 metres above sea level at 2 °S but some 27,600 metres above polar sea level.

Asimov also pointed out, however, that from a mountaineering point of view the critical issue is the thinness of the air and, in that respect, the peak of Everest has the lowest air pressure of any point on the earth's surface.

Mitchell Sandler, Edgware, Middx

Your respondents' details of different heights for Mt Everest are interesting, but one cannot compare them unless one knows the data to which they refer.

British Ordnance Survey maps give altitudes above mean sea level, averaged over a long period. For a small island this is fairly straightforward. I do not know what datum was used by the survey of India, or whether it was related to sea level. A complication is that the notional global mean sea level surface is not a simple spheroid, but has undulations of amplitude of 100 metres or so (the geoid of geophysicists). So altitudes referred to a local sea level for the Indian subcontinent would depend on where the sea level was determined.

All this ignores crustal movements that still affect the Himalayan range.

(Prof.) D. T. Donovan, Department of Earth Sciences,
University College London

The arbitrary selection of the variable datum of 'sea level' as a guide to a mountain's height obscures the fact that Mount Everest is far from the highest mountain in the world, being 1,355 metres shorter than the record holder.

Chimborazo in the Andes may claim a summit that is furthest from the centre of the earth, but Mauna Kea, part of the Big Island of Hawaii, stretches 10,203 m (33,476 ft) from its base on the floor of the Pacific to its peak 4,245 m (13,796 ft) above the sea.

On the same standardized measurement, Everest reaches 8,848 m and Chimborazo stands a mere 6,267 m tall. An interesting consequence of Isaac Asimov's conclusions, as described by Mitchell Sandler, is that the beaches of Ecuador are actually 'higher' (further from the centre of the earth) than the summit of Everest.

Robert Auger, Lympne, Kent

A recent TV programme showed excavation of an ancient Greek city on the Euphrates called Zeugma. According to the dictionary, the word means an obscure figure of speech. Is there any connection?

The ancient Greek word *zeugma* derives from the verb *zeugnymi*, which meant, among other things, 'to bridge a river'. In this context zeugma would mean 'bridge' and as a place name would therefore denote the existence of a bridge nearby. Zeugma was later used as a syntactical term and was subsequently adopted by the English language – 'a figure of speech in which a word is used to modify or govern two more words although appropriate to only one of them or making a different sense with each' (New Collins Dictionary) – i.e., in a syntactical context, a word acting as a bridge between two other words.

George Apostolakis, Leoforos, Greece

Zeugma is an ancient city located now in south-eastern Turkey that served as an important link for transporting timber from the Taurus mountains of Anatolia to the first literate, urban civilizations of Mesopotamia.

Zeugma was composed of twin cities named Seleucia and Apamea at either side of the river Euphrates and ruled by first Alexandria's Greek empire, then by the Roman empire, for several centuries beginning from the 300s BC.

(Dr) Lale Say, Edinburgh

How American is apple pie?

William Penn, an early father of America, had two aunts who owned a bakery in New England. Double-crusted fruit pies made with either apple or cherry were an American innovation, and sold like 'hotcakes' at the bakery. One year an early frost killed off the cherry crop, making the cost of cherry pies prohibitive. Consequently, the apple pie became more popular in the New England states, and eventually in all of America. So why is apple pie synonymous with America? Indubitably, it is due to the pie rates of Penn's aunts!

Beverlee McIntosh, Ottawa, Canada

Populations around the world often refer to their 'motherland'. Is it only Germans who use the term 'fatherland', and if so, why?

'Fatherland' is widespread in most Western languages. The Romans had a 'fatherland' – *patria*, from *pater*, father, from which is derived the vocabulary of 'patriotism' in English and other European languages. The term is translated directly into French as *patrie*, into German as *Vaterland*, and into Russian as *otechestvo* (*otets* being Russian for 'father'). However, *patria* is a feminine noun, as are the proper names of many countries, which are also often embodied by female allegorical figures. In French, *la patrie* is a feminine noun, literally meaning 'the fatherland', but is symbolically represented by Marianne. In Russian, *otechestvo*, a neuter noun, seems to have gained currency in the reign of Peter I. He took the Roman-style title 'Father of the Fatherland' (Otets Otechestva). An older Russian term is *rodina*, which is feminine, more folksy and closely linked with the land (*rod*) and the people (*narod*). Mat'-Rodina, 'Motherland', is thus the symbolic figure one sees in the large Russian memorials to the Second World War – which is nevertheless called 'the Great War for the Fatherland'.

M. Gilchrist, Cupar, Fife

Icelanders speak of their country as 'fatherland'. For some reason, they also use this word to mean 'long johns', especially those knitted from a rather coarse (to my wimpish sensibilities) wool.

Andrew Cauthery, Haslemere, Surrey

The French get the best of both worlds with *la mère patrie*: Mother Fatherland!

Charles Wilson, Eysines, France

In Polish we use both terms. There is a motto in Polish – 'God, Honour and the Fatherland'. We also speak of our 'mother tongue' and quite often interchange 'motherland' and 'fatherland' when speaking about Poland. Both are equally important.

Tom Dmochowski, London W4

It's not just the Germans. Here in Wales our national anthem celebrates *'Mae Hen Wlad Fy Nhadau'* – The Land of My Fathers.

Andy Roberts, Cardiff

A quick check through *National Anthems of the World* (1978 edition) revealed that the equivalent of fatherland was used in Austria, Bolivia, Brazil, Cameroon, Central African Republic, Chile, Costa Rica, Cuba, Ecuador, El Salvador, France, Gabon, Germany (both East and West), Guinea-Bissau, Haiti, Honduras, Ivory Coast, Liechtenstein, Mexico, Monaco, Mozambique, The Netherlands, Peru, Portugal, Romania, Switzerland, Uruguay, Wales and (if the translation is to be believed) Algeria, North Korea, Lesotho, Lithuania, Malagasy, Tunisia and Vietnam.

Of the non-English anthems, the idea of motherland only appeared in the anthems of Bangladesh, Greenland, Indonesia, Malta, Sabah and Sri Lanka.

Tom McCanna, Sheffield

In ancient Rome how much world geography was known? Did they have a word for China? How much of Africa had they explored?

We should assume that the existence of the Americas was completely unknown to the classical world. As for China, silk was a luxury fabric in ancient Rome and its inhabitants were well aware that it came from somewhere far to the east. Through the efficient trade secrecy of the Middle Eastern and Central Asian middlemen monopolizing the traffic in silk and spices along the 'Silk Road', Rome had no more than shadowy information about the source of this commodity or any of the contemporaneous civilizations of the Far East. I am unaware of any name in Latin for China during the classical period.

As for Africa, of the continent's interior only the territories of the Axumite civilization in modern-day Ethiopia and Eritrea were known by Greek (and perhaps Roman) traders and settlers, who reached this area by sailing south down the Red Sea from Egypt.

In AD 65, the emperor Nero dispatched a legion up the

Nile in search of the source, but it was defeated by the swamps of the Sudd, 1,000 miles upstream from Egypt. But a mystery remains. Ptolemy of Alexandria, the celebrated astronomer and geographer of the first century AD, proclaimed that the source of the Nile was to be found in large lakes deep in the interior that were fed by the snows of mighty mountains. Ptolemy's second-hand source was a Greek trader called Diogenes, who had apparently set off into the interior from the port of Rhapta (probably near modern-day Dar es Salaam on the East African coast). He had described seeing huge lakes and high snow-capped mountains after a journey of twenty-five days.

In the second half of the nineteenth century, the travels of Burton, Speke, Grant, Stanley and others seemed to substantiate much of Ptolemy's assertions. Victorian classical scholars were quick to identify the Ruwenzori range (on the modern Congo–Uganda border) and its snow peaks and glaciers (whose melting waters did indeed feed into the Nile system) with Ptolemy's mountains, and his lakes with the vast inland seas recently named after Queen Victoria and Prince Albert. All in all, though, it appears that Ptolemy was probably guessing (if, indeed, in an inspired way) and that Diogenes was probably something of a fraud. In his day, it would have taken a great deal longer than twenty-five days to reach the great lakes, and much longer still to reach the Ruwenzori range. And the difficulties posed by such a journey then would probably have been insurmountable.

Stephen Bell, Newark, Notts

The Romans knew the coasts of Africa from what is now Morocco in the west to Somalia in the east, and also discovered the Nile springs. They circumnavigated Scotland and reached the Baltic Sea, though they considered Scandinavia to be an island. North-western India was known quite well, and they had some information about south India and south-east Asia. Sri Lanka was known as Taprobane and Malaya as the Golden Peninsula. The Latin word for China was Serica, meaning 'Silk Country'. That they actually reached it is known from the Chinese annals that record a trade delegation from Rome in AD 168.

Claus Hollenberg, Marburg, Germany

In his *Achievements of the Divine Augustus*, Augustus Caesar states: '27.1. I added Egypt to the empire of the Roman people' and '31.1. From kings in India embassies were frequently sent to me, which before that time had not been seen with any Roman leader' (*Res Gestae Divi Augusti*, Brunt and Moore, OUP, 1967).

Nick Zair, Bristol

A very interesting account of Libya (Africa) is found in Herodotus' *Histories*, concerning the circumnavigation of

Africa by the Egyptian king Neco. Herodotus believed that Europe was larger than Africa and Asia combined. Neco sent an expedition down the Red Sea to sail southwards and round Africa, stopping for provisions on the way. In the third year they returned to Egypt via the Pillars of Hercules.

The fact that Herodotus did not believe their story actually vouches for its authenticity. He writes: 'These men made a statement which I do not myself believe, though others may . . . that as they sailed round the southern end of Libya, they had the sun on their right – to the north of them.'

Paul D. Oldfield, Northwich, Cheshire

Does the Rubicon still exist?

The Rubicon is a small stream rising in the foothills of the Etruscan Apennines to enter the Adriatic Sea at the resort of Gatteo a Mare, some ten miles north of Rimini. It formed the southern boundary of the province of Cisalpine Gaul with the Roman Republic, and so its crossing by Julius Caesar in January 49 BC was effectively a declaration of war on his rival, Pompey, who commanded the armies of the Roman senate. The stream's identity was once a source of some dispute, the Uso, the Piscatello and the Fiumicino di Savignano all being the subjects of rival claims. The Uso was awarded the name by a Papal Bull of 1756, but a comparison of distances with the accounts of Suetonius, Plutarch and Lucan led to the Fiumicino being officially renamed the Rubicon in 1932.

James Elliot, British Library Map Library, London WC1

Nowadays travellers in this part of the world are better catered for than Julius Caesar was in 49 BC when he crossed the Rubicon, as they can stop off for a snack at the Rubicone service station on the A14 autostrada between the Cesna and Rimini interchanges.

Keith Spence, Tunbridge Wells, Kent

Did any member of an Indian tribe ever say 'White man speak with forked tongue' or was this an invention of Hollywood?

James Adair, in his *History of the American Indians* (1755), writes of their condemnation of European 'speakers who use their squint eyes and forked tongues like the chieftains of the snakes'. This may have been prompted by the missionary preaching of George Whitefield, the Methodist, whose cross-eyes earned him the nickname of Doctor Squintus, and whose stay in North America coincided with that of Adair.

J. L. Wood, London, NW11

When did the expression 'Russian roulette' first come into use? Why Russian? Are there authenticated cases of it being played?

Russian roulette may have its origins in *A Hero of Our Time* by Mikhail Lermontov (1814–41) where he tells of a Lieutenant Vulich whose only passion was for cards, which he usually lost – and most of his money at that. When an argument arose about predestination, he maintained there was no such thing and backed his belief with a wager of 200 roubles. He was taken up on the bet whereupon he walked to a wall with weapons hanging on it and at random took one of the pistols. He poured powder into the touchpan and asked the pistol's owner – a major – if the pistol was loaded. The owner didn't remember. Vulich held the pistol to his head and pulled the trigger. It misfired. Some of the onlookers said it wasn't loaded. Vulich cocked the gun again, aimed at a cap hanging over the window and a bullet pierced its centre.

S. Kaufman, Ilford, Essex

There is a wealth of fictional references, notably the nineteenth-century Russian writer, Ossendowski, in his unforgettable *Man And Mystery In Asia*. But the most well-documented factual example is surely Graham Greene's experience of at least six episodes. One took place (summer 1924 to January 1925) while he was up at Oxford:

I would walk out from Headington towards Elsfield
. . . a sodden unfrequented country lane; the revolver
would be whipped behind my back, the chamber
twisted, the muzzle quickly inserted in my ear
beneath the black winter trees, the trigger pulled . . .

Evidence was left behind in the form of free verse permanently on his desk 'so that if I lost the gamble, it would
provide incontrovertible evidence of an accident, and my
parents, I thought, would be less troubled by a fatal play-
acting than a suicide'.

John Bray, Haywards Heath, West Sussex

**The Cynics were a sect started in ancient Greece by
Diogenes. Why were they called Cynics instead of
Diogenics?**

Diogenes was not the founder of the Cynic sect but
merely the best-known member of it. The Cynics traced
their origin to Antistheses, one of Socrates' companions,
and thence to Socrates himself. Cynic doctrine emphasized that individual virtue and happiness could be
attained only by a rejection of the world and its conventions, and this was exemplified in the way of life followed
by members of the school. It was apparently because of
their uninhibited 'natural' behaviour that the Cynics
acquired their name, which is equivalent to the Greek

word for 'dog', an epithet applied to them by those out-
raged by Cynic immodesty. Diogenes seems to have
accepted this nickname with equanimity, and, according
to a contemporary account, a marble dog was placed over
his grave. Presumably the modern meaning of 'cynic' has
developed from the Greek Cynics' tendency to distrust
outward show and to attempt to dispel men's illusions
wherever possible.

Michael Rendell, Poole, Dorset

**Is it true that King Juan Carlos of Spain is also
King of Jerusalem? If so, how did the title come
about, and what powers does it confer?**

While it is true that there is still a titular king of
Jerusalem, the title is held by Otto von Habsburg, not the
present king of Spain. It originates from the conquest of
the Holy Land by the first crusade in 1099. Godfroi de
Bouillon became ruler of Jerusalem, then his brother,
Baudouin, became king proper, on Godfroi's death, in
1100. As with many regal titles, the kingship survived the
loss of the land to which it pertained (Queen Elizabeth II
is still Duke of Normandy). The 'kingship' of Jerusalem
passed through French noble families and was held by the
House of Lorraine. The title passed into the Habsburg
dynasty when Francis de Lorraine married Maria Theresa

of Austria, and so also became Holy Roman Emperor. The Austrian Habsburgs are very much alive today, even if denuded of empire.

Ian Morland, Warrington, Cheshire.

The Alamo is often portrayed as a fight to the death by the defenders. But I read somewhere that there were survivors, and that Davy Crockett lived on to become a congressman. What is the true story?

The questioner is nearly correct: there were survivors and Davy Crockett did serve a term as a US congressman – but that was some years before the Alamo. Crockett's term as a congressman for Tennessee was not a howling success, and he did not seek re-election. He quickly returned to his old adventuring life, and, upon word of the Mexican invasion of the Republic of Texas, gathered a band of his frontiersman cronies and headed west in search of a good fight.

His arrival at the Alamo was purely fortuitous, and was a source of irritation to both the Texan commanders of the Alamo, Colonel Buck Travis and Colonel Jim Bowie (he of Bowie knife fame), themselves already at logger-heads over who was in overall command. Crockett did not submit to even the Texan style of quasi-military discipline and, to the fury of Travis, kept conducting raids on the Mexican forces without bothering to inform his fellow defenders. The defenders of the Alamo fought to the death. They were spurred on to do so by an incident earlier in the campaign, when General Santa Ana's forces had surrounded a Texan infantry battalion under the command of Colonel Fannin and forced them to surrender at Goliad. Most of Fannin's men were then massacred by the Mexicans.

When Santa Ana's troops surrounded the Alamo, Travis and Bowie adamantly refused to surrender. Travis, Bowie and Crockett were all killed, and the last half-dozen or so defenders who did surrender or were captured were dragged out and bayonetted to death by the Mexican infantry.

The survivors were all non-combatants, mostly of Spanish descent, who had taken refuge in the Alamo before the siege. An excellent account of the Alamo can be found in *Deaths Of The Bravos*, by John M. Myers, which draws on many contemporary accounts.

Morgen Witzel, Leigh, Kent

After the battle, Crockett's body, along with his famous (if environmentally unsound) coonskin hat, was identified by Mrs Dickinson, an officer's wife and one of the few occupants of the Alamo to survive.

Despite this, a Walt Disney 'bio-pic' (accompanied, I

seem to recall, by that thigh-slapping acid house forerunner, 'The Ballad of Davy Crockett') questioned
whether he had actually died, but this was just wishful
thinking.

Among the 183 defenders, only Brigido Guerrero, a
local man, survived – by managing to convince the
Mexicans that he had been a prisoner of the Texans.

One soldier escaped before the battle: Louis Rose, a
French Napoleonic veteran.

Rose appears to have been the only one whose professional experience allowed him to see what was coming
and leave the keen amateurs to get on with it. His reward
was a permanent place in Texan folklore as (you've
guessed it) the 'Yellow Rose of Texas'.

Brendan Morrissey, Haslemere, Surrey

**I have read that the Founding Fathers of America
opted for English over German as the official
language by only one vote. Is this true?**

I think the questioner has come across a variation on the
'Muhlenberg legend', which normally tells of how, during
the American War of Independence, Congress met to
decide whether English would continue as the official
language of their new country after opposition had
been raised by the many German and Dutch settlers in

Pennsylvania. It is said that German, French and Hebrew were all considered.

The story stems from a much simpler request from a group of German businessmen in Virginia that some laws might be issued in German as well as English, but with no intention of changing the overall linguistic status quo. It is this proposal that was rejected by one vote, cast by Frederick Muhlenberg, himself a German speaker.

Paul Mennim, Edinburgh

Is there any evidence to suggest that the Soviet Union ever contemplated the possibility of making a military assault on Western Europe?

According to secret documents seized from the military archives of the former East Germany, the Warsaw Pact planned a modernized version of Hitler's Blitzkrieg against the West, using spearheads of tanks and tactical nuclear weapons. These documents, covering the period from the sixties to the mid-eighties, were made public in March of this year [1994]. They convinced German military planners and historians that the Soviet bloc not only seriously considered an assault, but also had achieved a far higher level of readiness than Western intelligence had assumed.

The Warsaw Pact intended to push forward on five

fronts to reach the French border in thirteen to fifteen days, according to the documents. Having conquered West Germany and the Low Countries, Soviet-bloc forces would then push through France to reach the Spanish border and the Atlantic coast within 30 to 35 days. A training exercise in 1980 developed a strategy for supporting the advance of the first front with 840 tactical nuclear weapons (targeted on Schleswig-Holstein, East Lower Saxony, North Hessen and East Bavaria). Warsaw Pact exercises were offensive and rarely practised defence against a Nato attack, as this was regarded as unlikely by the East's military planners.

Soviet-bloc planning for a military offensive against the West was so detailed and advanced that the communists had already made street signs for Western cities, printed cash for their occupation government and built equipment to run Eastern trains on Western tracks. Furthermore, an estimated 8,000 medals ready for an offensive against the West were discovered in the former East German defence ministry headquarters. This secret decoration for bravery was known as the Blücher Order, after the Prussian field marshal who helped Wellington to defeat Napoleon at Waterloo.

Tony Martin, Nunhead, London SE15

As is usual in anti-Soviet stories, Tony Martin does not enable us to check the authenticity of his sources (which in any case should be Soviet, not German, to hold any water).

My fascination with this question began when we re-armed Germany in 1951, to the great dismay of our former ally – Germany being a power that had twice been our mortal enemy and that had spread death, destruction and genocide across Europe and Russia on an unprece-dented scale.

In my compulsive quest for information, I failed to find one piece of cast-iron, irrefutable evidence that the Soviet Union could have contemplated such a step. They lost 20 million, plus countless wounded, which must have left cruel mental scars on the surviving population.

Material destruction was on a scale unimaginable, even to those of us who remember the bombing of our cities. The Soviet Union was striving to prove the superiority of a planned economy. One can hardly imagine them being diverted into military gambles.

Mr Martin could not quote a single Russian leader from Lenin onwards who ever nursed such an idea.

The reverse is true: the West did contemplate an assault on the Soviet Union, from John Foster Dulles and his 'Roll back Communism' through to Reagan's 'Star Wars', which, it was hoped, would allow a successful first strike.

As stated by A. J. P. Taylor in *The Russian War 1941–45* (1978): 'The greatest crime of the Soviet Union in Western eyes is to have no capitalists and no landlords.'

Now that these are being reinstated we can be buddies.

Incidentally, they have been running through-trains from Moscow to Ostend and return for many years. They simply crane up the coaches and change the bogies at the frontier.

John L. Beasley, Penzance, Cornwall

What became of the *Terra Nova*, Scott's ship on his disastrous polar expedition?

The *Terra Nova* was built in 1884 as a whaling ship, but became better known as a polar expedition ship. She served with the Jackson-Harmsworth expedition of 1894–7, as relief ship for Scott's Discovery expedition in 1903, and returned to the Antarctic with Scott's 1910–13 expedition.

She was repurchased by her previous owners, Bowring Brothers Ltd, in 1913 and from 1914 to 1942 was based in Nova Scotia. She served in the seasonal Newfoundland seal fishery during the months of March and April, but was generally laid up for the rest of the year.

During the First World War she also made some coastal trading voyages with cargoes from Canada's Maritime Provinces to St John's, Newfoundland, and at least one voyage to Cardiff, with pitprops.

In 1942 she was chartered to carry supplies for US

bases in Greenland. On Sunday 12 September that year, while on passage from Greenland to Newfoundland, she developed a bad leak and at 19:20 hours transmitted an SOS message. This was answered by the US coastguard cutter *Atak*, which, by daybreak next day, had picked up the crew of twenty-four men from the *Terra Nova*, by now sinking and burning. The master of the *Terra Nova* was the last man to board the *Atak*, which then ensured her sinking with twenty-three rounds of 3" gun fire. Her approximate last position was 60' 30 °N 46' 30 °W, off the south-western coast of Greenland.

Iain MacKenzie, Maritime Information Centre,
Greenwich, London SE10

What is the origin of the term 'Third World'?

The term comes from the 'original' world (i.e. the Middle East, Mediterranean Europe, mainland Europe, British Isles) being termed the 'Old World' when the 'New World' (i.e. the Americas) was settled by Europeans.

This left the rest of the world (i.e. Africa, Asia, etc.), which was renamed the 'Third World' in the latter part of this century.

David A. Dix, Newcastle-under-Lyme,
Staffs

I have always thought the term originates from the car insurance industry. In a car accident, the innocent victim is called the third party. Thus 'Third World' refers to the idea that it is an innocent victim of a collision between the capitalist First World and the communist Second World.

John Anderton, Weaverham, Cheshire

I disagree with Mr Dix's explanation. The term is a translation from the French *Tiers-Monde* created by the late economist and demograph, Alfred Sauvy. Modelled after the *Tiers-Etat* of the pre-1789 era (meaning those who weren't aristocrats or church members). The *Tiers-Monde* was applied to those countries who weren't part of the Western world (which the English renamed the First World) or the communist world. The term had a wide success because, just as the *Tiers-Etat* was the power behind the French Revolution, the Third World could become a new revolutionary actor. Since these times, a new term, the *Quart-Monde* (Fourth World) has appeared in France, and it comprises all those who are poor in rich countries (unemployed, tramps, etc.).

Xavier Leroy, Johannesburg, South Africa

Your correspondent Xavier Leroy has the right translation of Third World as coming from the French *Tiers-Monde*. However, I think he misunderstands the actual English

meaning of it. *Tiers* means third in the sense of 'the fraction one-third', not in the sense of 'third in a sequence'.
Thus, by inference, *le tiers monde* means the third of the
world that does not enjoy the same standard of living as
the remaining two-thirds. There are thus no First or
Second Worlds.

D. R. Allum, Towcester, Northants

**'Early music' in the catalogues dates from the
Middle Ages. Is there nothing earlier? Did the
Greeks and Romans, for example, write musical
scores? If so, what happened to them?**

Evidence of ancient music abounds – ancient Egyptian
wall paintings depict harp-playing as early as the tenth
century BC. A horn similar to those used in fox hunting
was buried with Tutankhamun and it can still be played.
In spite of this, it is impossible to reconstruct the music
that was played on it.

As for the Greeks, there are numerous references in surviving texts, such as those written by Aristoxenus of
Tarentum, Claudius Ptolemy and Aristide Quintilianus.
These tell us about music in the same way that a newspaper music critic might review a new record. It is equivalent
to future generations trying to reconstruct a symphony
from the *Guardian*'s music critic.

There is even less hard information about Roman music, although the fact that the Roman Catholic Church is the direct descendant of the Roman Empire gives us some clues. The earliest surviving Western music is liturgical. The Gregorian chant, named after Pope Gregory I (540–604), is a musical link with Antiquity. As for the Classical scores, the ancients did have a notation but only fragments have survived. These are too short to give any clue as to how ancient music sounded.

Peter Stockhill, Middlesbrough, Cleveland

Why did Hitler not invade Switzerland?

Because a stable, working Switzerland served him better, providing a base for business deals, an important railway link to Italy, a safe haven for spies and securing diplomatic contact with enemy forces. 'Six days a week Swiss work for Hitler, on the seventh they pray for victory of the Allied forces,' went a joke in those times. The German share of Swiss exports (mainly weapons, ammunition, high-tech machinery and food) increased from 15.5 per cent to 42 per cent between 1937 and 1942.

Not only civil goods made their way from or to Germany through Switzerland: weaponry was transported up to October 1941, and forced Italian labour as late as 1943. The Allied forces even considered bombing the

Gotthard line in 1944. Money robbed by the Nazis during the war was transferred into Swiss bank accounts. Although aware of the fate of those fleeing the death camps in Germany, the Swiss authorities refused to take in more people. Germany really had no reason for invading Switzerland, as this country worked so well for the Nazis. If there was a winner in the Second World War, it was the Swiss.

Thomas Schwager, Saint Gallen, Switzerland

Can anyone provide information about the fire at Alexandria in Egypt that destroyed the great library there among other things? When was it, do we know what was lost, and what were the consequences?

The library was the first research institute in world history. Alexander the Great's successors as ruler of Egypt, Ptolemy I and II, developed it in the third century BC. It contained the greatest collection of handwritten papyrus scrolls in the ancient world, perhaps numbering over 700,000, and a foundation for the systematic study of the arts and sciences was established. Even the Old Testament came down to us from mainly Greek translations made in the library.

The library was deliberately burnt down by a mob

c. AD 420 as classical civilization disintegrated and the Dark Ages closed in. All that survived was a tiny fraction of its work and a cellar of the Serapaeum, the library annexe. The loss was incalculable but we do know, for example, that the work of Eratosthenes, a library director who had accurately calculated the size of the Earth, and Aristarchus of Samos, who had postulated a heliocentric universe, the axis-rotation of the Earth and its revolution around the Sun, had to be rediscovered by Columbus and Copernicus a thousand years later. Of the 123 plays of Sophocles only seven survived (one of which was *Oedipus Rex*). Much the same happened to the work of Aeschylus and Euripides.

Tony Martin, London SE15

I have just been told that the people of Iceland enjoy the highest standard of living in the world. Can anyone confirm this?

In Iceland they have a truly classless society where people build their dream homes on their own land. Reykjavik is a completely smokeless city where homes are heated by water from the natural hot springs and electricity is produced by vast hydroelectric schemes – one of the cheapest ways of utilizing natural resources to create power. I understand that unemployment is virtually unknown, the economy is dependent on the fishing industry and all education is free. Iceland is also one of the most literate countries in the world – Reykjavik boasts more bookshops per head of population than any other city.

Ruth Booth, London SE4

What are the destinations in the song 'Route 66' by Them, and what exactly does Van Morrison sing after 'Flagstaff, Arizona, don't forget Winona'.

The words of the song, written by Bob Troup and published in 1946, tell it all:

It winds from Chicago to LA,
More than two thousand miles all the way.
Get your kicks on Route 66!
Now you go thro' Saint Looey [sic] and Joplin, Missouri
And Oklahoma City is mighty pretty
You'll see Amarillo; Gallup, New Mexico; Flagstaff, Arizona;
Don't forget Winona, Kingman, Barstow, San Bernardino . . .

'Have your fun on the A41' somehow does not have the same ring to it:

It winds from London to Birkenhead,
Just over two hundred miles like I said.
Have some fun on the A41

Now you bypass Chester, Warwick and Bicester,
Birmingham City is jolly pretty
You'll see Hemel Hempsted Waddesdon, Berkhamsted too.
Tring, Banbury, don't forget Aylesbury,
Bicester, Watford and Wolverhampton . . .

Ah well, back to the day job.

Clive Ablett, Berkhamsted, Herts

Gutzon Borglum, the American sculptor, was famous for his monumental busts of US presidents on Mount Rushmore. How did he carry out this work and when?

Borglum, who had studied at the Beaux-Arts in Paris, began by sculpting the four torsos in miniature. He and his assistants then mapped the models by suspending a weighted string from a horizontal rod, which they rotated above the miniatures. By measuring the distance between the string and numerous key points on the heads, they produced a precise (notionally) three-dimensional grid, showing exactly where everything should be. These measurements, of which there were thousands, were then multiplied to produce a version of the grid gigantic enough to fit the mountain. To locate the key points on the granite rockface, Borglum's team measured the distance back from ropes suspended from a series of protruding poles fixed above. Despite its crudeness, this method proved very successful. Using a system of drilling and blasting, the heads were hewn from the rock. At one point the head of Jefferson had to be rotated slightly to his left when a vertical fault was discovered in the granite. This fault now runs visibly down the right side of the nose, the nostril of which is, incidentally, big enough to sleep in. Work on the 60 ft-high structure was stopped in 1941, the year Borglum died. By that time many people were sick of the delays, accidents and infighting. The monument was never finished, and if you visit Mount Rushmore today you can just see Lincoln's fingers starting to emerge from the granite, at the point where the work was abruptly halted.

Charles Mutto, London SW1

He started to deface Mount Rushmore on 4 October 1927. By 31 October 1941, the defacement was complete. The site for this sculpture is in the centre of Sioux Indian sacred land, the Paha Sapa (the Black Hills), ceded to the Sioux nation in perpetuity in 1868. It is said that Borglum wanted to carve full-length figures of the presidents but died before their completion. Perhaps if he had started at the presidents' feet, instead of their heads, Americans would have a more appropriate 'shrine' to their democracy.

(Ms) Kim Hopkins (Cherokee Indian), London W5

What was the good news that they brought from Ghent to Aix?

Aix is besieged and about to surrender; the good news is that help is on the way. This is the implied meaning of line 46 of Robert Browning's poem, 'the news which alone could save Aix from her fate'. The explanation is Browning's, but he gave it with reluctance; he always insisted that the ride itself was what mattered. He said that he wrote the poem 'on board ship off Tangiers', when he 'had been at sea long enough to appreciate even the fancy of a gallop'. There is no historical foundation for the episode: according to Browning it reflects a 'general impression of the characteristic warfare and besieging that abounds in the annals of Flanders'.

D. Karlin (co-editor, with John Woolford, of The Poems of Browning, *Longman Annotated English Poets, 1991)*

Is there a difference between Holland and the Netherlands; if so, what is it?

It is rather like the difference between England and Britain. The Netherlands is divided into twelve provinces, two of which are North Holland and South Holland, containing Amsterdam, Den Haag (the Hague) and Rotterdam. Properly, the other Dutch provinces – such as

Utrecht or North Brabant – are not part of Holland, only part of the Netherlands.

This confusion (between England and Britain, Holland and the Netherlands) is made by other Europeans, too: a French person will typically refer to anyone from Britain as '*anglais*', and to anyone from the Netherlands as '*hollandais*'.

Ian O'Neill, Whiteparish, Wilts

Further to Ian O'Neill's reply: in the sixteenth and seventeenth centuries, when the Dutch were a great seafaring people, all the Netherlands' main ports were located in either north or south Holland. So sailors on their travels would explain that they came from Holland.

F. Kok, Lincoln

Were Native Americans' smoke signals myth or fact? If fact, what range of information could they convey?

The book *Indian Sign Language* by William Tomkins (Dover) uses as its source the Museum of the American Indian in New York City:

Inasmuch as they aimed to transmit secret knowledge, most or many of the signs were devised privately and to suit a particular purpose or the caprice of the transmitter.

There were, however, certain more or less recognized abstract smoke signals . . . One puff meant 'Attention'. Two puffs meant 'All's well'. Three puffs of smoke, or three fires in a row, signifies 'Danger', 'Trouble' or a call for help.

Margaret B. Brooks, Pittsburgh, US

How long after the American Revolution and the War of 1812 did it take for Britain and the United States to become friends again?

The questioner should first make the distinction between friendship and alliance. The burning of the White House, and the Cotton Kings' support of the South in the Civil War, still rankle in Washington. The Americans may have been our allies, to their profit, in two world and numerous minor wars in the past 100 years, but they are not necessarily our friends.

J. S. Bain, Stromness, Orkney

After the War of 1812 many believed that another Anglo–American war was possible. The British possessions in Northern America were a continuing source of tension. Many Americans wanted to annex them while British prime ministers from Wellington to Palmerston saw it as their duty to defend them. Thus more, and stronger, border forts were built in British North America in the half-century after 1815 than in any other period.

While defensive schemes were put in place, border disputes with the US were frequent. First there were clashes between Maine and New Brunswick, then disputes in Oregon and on the Pacific coast. Most serious were the tensions during the Civil War, when the North's conviction that Great Britain sympathized with the Confederacy led to uneasy relations between the two countries.

But in 1871 an Anglo–American accord, the Treaty of Washington, liquidated these tensions. At the same time Britain completed the withdrawal of its troops from North America except for small garrisons left at Halifax and Esquimalt. Complementing these moves was the consolidation of the British North American provinces into the Dominion of Canada. Tacitly, the United States accepted that a separate and stable new entity had emerged to its north. The Canadian–American boundary was gradually demilitarized. The way was now open for Canada, the US and Britain to move, with only minor setbacks, to friendship and later to alliance.

David Farr, Ottawa, Canada

Helsingor (Hamlet's Elsinore); Helsingborg in

Sweden; Helsinki (also known as Helsingfors) – what's the connection?

The common factor in Scandinavia's Helsing-names is *hals*, meaning 'neck', and they refer to areas belonging to people located at the throttle point of a strait or sound. So had the Vikings had their way even more completely, Dover and Calais might have been called Elsinore and Helsingborg.

Clemens Ostergaard, University of Aarhus, Denmark

I have heard that, at some time in the past, people in China paid their doctor regularly while they remained well. When they became sick, payment was suspended on the basis that the doctor had failed to keep them healthy. Is this story true? Could it be adapted to the NHS?

The Chinese system of only paying doctors while they remained well was not only true but thrives in the NHS today. As a matter of government policy there has been a steady increase in the proportion of GPs' pay derived from capitation (that is payment per patient on the doctors list). This means that I can receive 60 per cent of my gross income even if I never have to see a patient. The moment I have to do so it costs me money in ancillary staff pay, heating and lighting my surgery, petrol and wear and tear on my car, etc. It is therefore in my interest to cure my patient promptly so that he or she does not have to be seen again. However, this is usually lost on those patients denied a prescription for the antibiotics they think they need for their common cold.

(Dr) John Davies, Kirby in Cleveland, North Yorks

In 1984, in the Gaoyi county of the Shijiazhuang prefecture, a plan was introduced to increase the uptake of vaccination programmes and enhance preventative measures against childhood illnesses. At that time, the average family income there was estimated to be about £120 p.a. Parents paid about £3.50 to the health authorities in the first year of their child's life in a contract to 'guarantee' the child would not contract measles, polio, whooping cough, tetanus or diphtheria, provided they received the full immunization programme. This premium was then used to pay for vaccination equipment, education and 'bonuses' amongst the local doctors and health centres. Should a child then suffer from measles or whooping cough, the parents were paid about £14 in compensation, and about £82 if they suffered from polio, diphtheria or tetanus. However, in the first two years, although almost £27,500 had been collected in premiums, only just over £200 had been paid out in compensation. The system worked because it served to stimulate healthcare staff to implement vaccination programmes; it enabled these staff to earn up to 50 per cent extra on their regular income as bonuses; and parents, having paid out a large portion of their income, were keen to have their children vaccinated.

Ian Shaw (virologist), Bromborough, Wirral

A number of countries are listed on the pediment of the Victoria and Albert Museum that overlooks the inner courtyard. One of these is Zoilverein but where is this?

The correct term is 'Zollverein', being a customs (*zoll*) union (*verein*). The Zollverein were established to encourage free trade amongst German states, primarily Prussia. One was established in 1834 that included most chief German states except Austria. A closer union was formed in 1867, the administration of which subsequently merged with that of the new German empire of 1871.

John Suett, London SW6

The straight-line division of American states created a small nib of land south of Tsawwassen near Vancouver. No Americans can access it without going through Canada and then re-entering

US territory via a small customs post. What is its purpose?

The 'nib of land' is Point Roberts, Washington. It was cut off from the rest of the United States by the 1846 Treaty of Washington, which drew the international boundary at the 49th parallel. The boundary continues along the parallel until it reaches the middle of the Juan de Fuca Strait, then goes south around Vancouver Island. There wasn't a permanent customs station until as late as the 1940s so Point Roberts' separation presumably wasn't much of a burden for the locals. As for its purpose, it was probably just a matter of administrative convenience for the treaty-makers!

Chris Owen, London SW1

Most of the world's straight-line borders are in sparsely populated areas such as the Sahara, the deserts of central Asia, or between Canada and Alaska. Where such straight borders approach more populated areas, e.g. coastal areas, they deviate from a straight line and follow a more natural course: for example the Egypt–Libya border.

The US–Canada straight-line border is probably the most heavily such populated border in the world. When drawn up, the coastal area near Vancouver Island and Tsawwassen was sparsely populated and no one considered deviating the border to a more logical line, such as to the south of Point Roberts. The US–Canada border has another illogicality: the Lake of the Woods area between Minnesota and Manitoba where the Red Lake Indian Reservation, US territory, is cut off by this lake from the rest of the US.

There are many minor border illogicalities where a small part of the territory of state A looks as if it ought to belong to state B. Usually these are for historical reasons, e.g. Llivia (a Spanish enclave inside France), the Channel Islands, the Caprivi Strip in north-east Namibia, or the Wakhan Valley in north-east Afghanistan. The historical reason for these anomalies has long since gone, but it is much easier to leave well alone than to persuade a state to cede some territory for the sake of a neater map.

Hillary Shaw, School of Geography, University of Leeds

What are the respective origins of the words Kansas and Arkansas? And why don't they rhyme?

Both Kansas and Arkansas are named after Native American Indian tribes. Kansas is named after the Kansa tribe, who called themselves Ni-U-Ko'n-Ska, which means 'children of the middle waters'. Arkansas is named after the Quapaw tribe. The Quapaw were called Arkansa (meaning 'south wind') by the Algonkian-speaking Indians. The spelling and pronunciation of Arkansas are the result of a resolution passed by the state's General Assembly in 1881. Its two senators at the time were divided on the issue. One senator was always introduced as the senator from 'ARkanSAW' and the other as the senator from 'Ar-KANSAS.' The resolution declared that the state's name should be pronounced 'Arkansaw' in memory of the original native American inhabitants, but spelled Arkansas, in the French manner, as the French were the first Europeans to explore the area. (Sources: Kansas State Historical Society, Arkansas Secretary of State.)

Philip Sills, Plainsboro, New Jersey, US

If the natives of Afghanistan are Afghans, of Uzbekistan are Uzbeks and of Tajikistan are Tajiks, why are those of Pakistan not Paks?

The name of Pakistan, the Muslim-majority state created out of the partition of India following the end of the British Raj, consists of two elements, both derived from Persian: *Pak* and *stan*. The Persian language has exerted a powerful influence on all the languages of central and south Asia, and was the administrative language of India before the British Raj. *Pak* means 'pure' and *stan* is a suffix meaning 'land' or 'place of'. Thus, Pakistan can be translated as 'Land of the Pure' or 'Place of Purity', the purity in question being religious (Pakistan was the first state to

119

describe itself as an 'Islamic Republic'). To call someone 'Pak' (or 'Paki') is to call them 'pure'.

The Tajiks speak a dialect of Persian, whereas the Uzbeks are a Turkic people (Turkish *uz*, 'great' and *beg*, 'prince'). Accordingly, Tajikistan is 'Land of the Tajiks' and Uzbekistan is 'Land of the Uzbegs (or 'Land of the Great Prince'). Other 'stans' include Almanistan (Germany), Bulgharistan (Bulgaria) and Inglestan (England). Apartheid South Africa had 'Bantustans' – nominal 'homelands' for the countries' various 'Bantu' peoples – and the term has passed into English to refer to an unviable or inequitably divided state. The 'stan' suffix can also be applied to places other than countries; hence *mimaristan* (hospital) and *bustan* (garden: 'place of [nice] smells').

Mike Diboll, Rotherhithe, London SE16

Mike Diboll is right to say that *Pak* means 'pure' and *stan* is a suffix meaning 'land' or 'place of'. However, this is a coincidence. The official Pakistani government website says that, in 1933:

> a group of Muslim students at Cambridge, headed by Chaudhry Rehmat Ali, issued a pamphlet, *Now or Never*, in which, drawing letters from the names of the Muslim majority regions, they gave the nomen- clature of 'Pakistan' to the proposed State . . . Many

people believe that Pakistan only derives its meaning from the words that translate into Land of the Pure. However this is not the primary derivation but a secondary one.

C. R. Ali first wanted freedom for the five Muslim 'Indian' homelands in north-west British India . . . namely Punjab, Afghania, Kashmir, Sindh and Balochistan from British colonial rule, followed by their reintegration with the three Muslim 'Asian' homelands of Afghanistan, Iran and Tukharistan (P.A.K.I.S.T.A.N.).

John Dean, Headington, Oxford

During the Second World War, King George VI awarded the then colonial island of Malta the George Cross. Does this award have any meaning for the present independent Republic of Malta and its citizens?

Yes it does, and its continued inclusion on the Maltese flag (which has been around since 1090) contrasts with a once misguided attempt by the British to add a Union Jack to it. Incidentally, Malta was not a colony but a Protectorate from 1802 when the Maltese invited the British to stay after Nelson helped them to evict Napoleon's occupying troops. Of course, the George Cross means less to the younger generation, but even they acknowledge their mothers' and fathers' fortitude when they read the King's message in history class:

> To honour her brave people
> I award the George Cross
> To the Island Fortress of Malta
> To bear witness to a heroism and devotion
> That will long be famous in history.

A. P. Galea, Woking, Surrey

We hear of Native Americans, Aboriginals and others being dispossessed by European settlers, but this does not seem to have been an issue as the Russian state extended eastwards. Were indigenous peoples there more successfully integrated?

The Russian eastward expansion wasn't conflict free but was less devastating than colonial ventures in Australia and the Americas mainly because the settlers (not very numerous) were primarily farmers, and the indigenous peoples hunter-gatherers and stockbreeders; each side needed the other's skills, especially in organizing the lucrative fur trade.

Robin Milner-Gulland, professor of Russian and East European studies, University of Sussex, Brighton

There are two large indigenous groups, the Yakuts and the Komi, who have their own republics within eastern Russia; there are former nations such as Tuva in southern Siberia; and at least twenty-six ethnic groups – including the Evenks, the Nenets, the Entsy, the Khants and the Evens – numbering in total fewer than 200,000 people.

Ethnic diversity was to some extent nurtured in communist Russia, with cultural festivals celebrating the different traditions of indigenous people. But the communists also attempted to 'modernize and integrate' them into a larger Russian nation. Programmes included collectivization, resettlement, Russian language schooling, industrialization and exploitation of natural resources and land. Collectivization in particular is disastrous for nomadic peoples, who need to roam freely to feed their animals on sparse vegetation. You could call their integration 'successful' in that fewer than 10 per cent of the indigenous people are now nomadic, down from more than 70 per cent thirty years ago.

You can identify indigenous people even in Siberia's cities through both their traditional dress and their appearance. Traditional ways of life are still under threat from a range of sources, including logging, poaching and pollution. If the questioner wants more information, try the excellent Survival International website at www.survival.org.uk.

Nick Mayhew-Smith, London SW19

The replies published ignore the central fact of Russian history: its subjugation of the Tartars and other Muslim peoples. Ivan IV captured Kazan in 1552, but the local population is still half Tartar. The Crimea was free until 1771, but Stalin deported the local Tartars to Central Asia. Although some Kazakhs mutated into Cossacks, peoples not 'successfully integrated' include: Turkmens, Tajiks, Kirghiz, Uzbeks – and many nations of the Caucasus.

John Still, Surbiton, Surrey

Winston Churchill visited British troops in Egypt shortly before the battle of El Alamein in 1942. Since virtually the whole of Europe was under Nazi occupation and there was a serious U-boat threat at sea, how on earth did he get there?

According to volume 4 of Churchill's *The Second World War*, he flew in a long-range Liberator bomber, in which the bomb racks had been replaced by somewhat primitive-sounding passenger accommodation. The first stage of the journey was from RAF Lyneham in Wiltshire to Gibraltar, the second from Gibraltar on to Cairo, this latter involving a considerable detour over the desert so as to avoid the areas of conflict in north Africa. Upon reaching the Nile, the aircraft turned northwards and carried on until it reached Cairo. Both Spanish and Vichy French 'neutrality' were violated in the course of the latter flight, the Liberator and its escort flying over territory belonging to both countries.

This route was chosen over the far longer one commonly used in sending reinforcements to the Middle East, via West Africa and the Sudan, which would have taken five or six days and which, while it would have been farther from the scene of battle, would have exposed the premier to the risk of contracting tropical diseases.

Steve Dent, Bath

Further to Steve Dent's reply: on 10 August 1942 I was a member of 1434 Flight RAF at Quali Morgeh airfield just outside Tehran in Persia (as it was then) and we were informed that an important visitor was expected the next day. Four Liberator aircraft arrived – one named Commando 3 carrying Winston Churchill, on his way to Moscow for his first meeting with Stalin. He held talks with the Shah of Persia and on 18 August he returned and had meetings in Egypt just before the battles of El Alamein.

George Blows, Cambridge

After various meetings in Cairo, on 5 August, Churchill flew in a Dakota to inspect the Eighth Army at Alamein. After inspecting the troops with General Gott, Churchill flew back to Cairo. On 7 August, Gott was shot down and killed, flying into Cairo on the same route Churchill had taken, unescorted, two days earlier.

Basil Morgan, Uppingham, Rutland

My father was an RAF pilot during the war, and one of his more interesting duties was to form part of a fighter escort for Churchill on his way back to the UK from 'somewhere in north Africa'. He was not told until the last minute what the duty was going to be, and the rendezvous point was out over the Atlantic, where a very large RAF escort took over from an equally large USAF one. This was in 1944, when air superiority for the Allies was more assured, but the journey was still no doubt a risky one for any VIP.

Chris Barnett, Tokyo

If Rome wasn't built in a day, how long did it actually take?

Rome was founded in 753 BC. It is now nearing completion.

Glanville Price, Comins Coch, Aberystwyth

Archaeological evidence reveals Bronze Age (1700–1000 BC) settlements in the southern Tiber River valley on what would later be called the Palatine and Esquiline hills.

Villages of wooden huts inhabited by people using iron tools and weapons existed between 900 and 700 BC. The legendary founding of Rome by Romulus took place in 753 BC. What was part of the Latin League became subject to Etruscan kings from 650 to 509 BC, during which period the swampland below three of the hills was drained, creating what would become the Roman Forum. This effectively changed what were separate villages into a single urban unit, which was walled in after the Gallic invasion of 390 BC.

By the late Republican era (100 BC), buildings were made of brick and concrete (a Roman invention) and clad in marble (so the story goes) under Ottavian (the first emperor) between 27 BC and AD 14. The city had new, more extensive walls built under the emperor Aurelion (AD 270–5). The capital of the Western empire was moved to Milan thirty years later, so Rome was built in something like 1,000 years.

Martin Attwood, Orvieto, Italy

Whenever I used to remind my former hard-driving boss that Rome wasn't built in a day, he would reply: 'That's because I wasn't in charge of the project.'

Moira Biggins, Derby

Ad vitam aeternam, according to its motto.

Silvana Lachance, Montreal, Canada

In the football teams from Dortmund, Mönchengladbach, etc., what does Borussia stand for?

'Borussia' is the Latin term for 'Prussia'. Oddly enough, neither of the teams lies within what is commonly seen as Prussia (i.e. the region close to Berlin): Mönchengladbach is in the Rhineland, Dortmund in Westphalia. However, both regions fell under Prussian occupation after the Napoleonic wars and were the westernmost provinces of the Prussian kingdom throughout most of the nineteenth century.

'Borussia' is also the term for a female symbol of Prussia (Prussia as a woman, as Marianne is a symbol for France). This lady therefore is the 'patron' of the two football clubs. More appropriately (because it's in Prussia), a Berlin club is named Tennis Borussia Berlin, but despite spending ridiculous amounts of money, this club never succeeded in its challenge to make the first German league.

Wigan Salazar, Munich, Germany

This was lost on the English football commentator who came up with the line: 'Borussia Dortmund nil, Borussia Mönchengladbach nil, so a draw in that Borussia derby . . .'

Alan Murray, Leeds

It would appear that the meaning is not widely known in Germany. This question was asked on the German version of *Who Wants to be a Millionaire?* The candidate did not know and decided to ask the audience. Only a small percentage opted for the correct answer, with the majority believing that Borussia meant 'victorious'. Sadly, the candidate believed the audience.

Peter Ruddy, Berlin

Further to the previous replies, 'Bayern Munich' (i.e. 'Bavaria Munich) should not be confused with 'Bayer Leverkusen', Bayer being the chemical firm that first produced aspirin. Similar is 'Carl Zeiss Jena', originally the works team of the firm producing optical instruments. 'Eintracht' means 'concord, harmony', i.e. the equivalent of 'United', in Eintracht Braunschweig, Eintracht Frankfurt. 'Fortuna Dusseldorf' and 'Fortuna Koln' are named after the goddess of good fortune and success. 'Hertha Berlin' comes originally from a misreading of the German goddess 'Nerthus' – she was a goddess of fertility, and 'Werder Bremen' refers to land drained and secured by dikes adjoining the River Weser.

Simon Skeens, Macclesfield, Cheshire

We have 'the Middle East' and 'the Far East', but where is 'the Near East'? And what should

we call the area that covers India, Bangladesh, Nepal, etc.?

'Near East' is the old name for Asia between Turkey and India (i.e. the area west of the pride of the British Empire). After the Second World War, a more precise name was needed, so Israel and neighbouring Arab countries became known as the 'Middle East'. Of course, it all depends where you are standing; many years ago, on my first visit to India, I was surprised to hear All India Radio talking about the crisis in 'West Asia' – the Middle East from their standpoint. 'South Asia' is the name given to the sub-Indian subcontinent, plus Nepal, Sri Lanka, etc., to distinguish it from south-east Asia, formerly Indo-China.

Mike Broadbent, Luton, Beds

In the days before British military withdrawal from east of Suez, the RAF had three separate eastern commands: Far East Air Force; Air Force Middle East and Near East Air Force. The latter comprised, from what I recollect, bases on Cyprus, Malta and Gibraltar. NEAF HQ was based at RAF Episcopi, Cyprus. The building is still in use but has been re-designated as HQ Joint Services.

Tony Cummings (ret. squadron leader), Hough Green, Chester

Is it true that no two democracies have ever gone to war with each other?

Democracy is partly a matter of degree. Britain, France and Germany were all democracies in 1914. In all three countries a democratically elected legislature could have prevented the declaration of war.

Norman Moss, London W12

In 1812, with the Napoleonic war still raging, the United Kingdom went to war with the United States. The War of 1812 is notable for the burning down of the original White House, and because the main battle took place after peace had officially been agreed. But the fact that the franchise in each country was far from complete – women, slaves, working classes and others excluded on at least one side of the Atlantic – could certainly be used to disqualify either as a democracy.

David May, London SW19

In 1983, the US invaded Grenada, which had just held open and fair elections. Unfortunately for the people of Grenada, they had failed to elect a leader acceptable to America.

In fact, the US has a very bad record in going to war against other democracies. They declared war on Vietnam because that country was about to (democratically) elect a communist government. One might argue that the CIA-run coup that put General Pinochet in charge of Chile was another example of waging war against a democracy. The question is whether the US governmental system, in which running for office costs so much money that incumbents will almost inevitably end up in hock to big business, can really be described as 'democratic'.

Tony Green, Ipswich, Suffolk

True democracy does not yet exist, because it requires effective participation in the political arena and an enlightened, informed public.

Hayley Loughran, Bradford

A *Guardian* column once stated: 'Finland is not part of Scandinavia [which] comprises Norway, Sweden, Denmark and Iceland.' Precisely what is Scandinavia?

Scandinavia is different things to different people: there are even disputes as to the origin of the name. One old spelling has it as Scadinavia, from the nucleus *skad-* meaning darkness or shade; another suggestion is that it is derived from the southern Swedish province of Skane.

Strictly speaking, it is literally the Scandinavian peninsula, which only includes Norway and Sweden, and excludes Denmark, which is on the Jutland peninsula joined to Germany. Some geologists and geographers refer to Fennoscandia if they want to include Finland, as that country has very similar ancient rock types that have been heavily glaciated.

On the basis of language, it would have to include Norway, Sweden, and Denmark – who can all understand each other without interpreters – plus lands settled by the Vikings, such as Iceland and the Faroe Islands; but would this also bring in Greenland, even though Danish is gradually giving way to the Inuit language? Finland would not normally be included on a linguistic basis as Finnish is part of a totally different language group – the Finno-Ugrian, which is only related in this area to Samisk (usually known as Lapp to British people) and Estonian.

Roger Partridge, Scandinavia Philatelic Society,
Surbiton, Surrey

What were the social effects in the nineteenth century of opium in China and hashish in Egypt? How were these mass addictions stopped – or weren't they?

The social effects of opium smoking among all sections of the Chinese population were deleterious, so much so that the growing of the opium poppy, the production, distribution and smoking of opium was prohibited by imperial decree. The imperial government largely succeeded in preventing the production and distribution of Chinese opium but it was not able to stop people smoking it.

The Chinese demand for opium was supplied by British traders from India. By the 1830s over 25,000 chests (each containing 130 to 160 lbs) were smuggled into China each year. In 1839, the Chinese court sent Lin Xexu as special commissioner to Canton, the centre of the opium trade, to enforce prohibition. He ordered the surrender of all opium stocks and imprisoned the British merchants in their factories. Lin's actions precipitated the first Anglo–Chinese war, or first opium war.

John Davies, Department of History,
Liverpool Hope University

Why does the British press ignore Canada? Is it because we're so boring?

The assertion is preposterous. Why, I have before me a *Guardian* news item, 'British Gas Pulls Out Of Canada', from as recently as 20 November 1993.

Robert Matthews, Cambridge

Please can we discuss something more interesting?

Mark Iliff, Caversham, Berks

Far from it. You are not boring, but it seems that the citizens of Canada live in peace and harmony, and as they are not affected by power conflicts, racism or drugs the British press seems to ignore your country. As the saying goes: 'No news is good news' – so cheer up!

Harish & Chandni Shah, London N4

As an expatriate Canadian, I posed just this question on the BBC's *Points Of View* a couple of years ago, after a flippant joke about boring Canadians appeared on television. Apparently, the answer is 'Yes'. Emigration may ameliorate, but does not wholly resolve, this condition.

Larry Winger, Sparty Lea, Northumberland

As an Australian married to a Korean I can say that we feel equally ignored. How many more areas of London do we need to occupy, how many more newspapers do we have to buy up, how many more electronic or automotive industries do we have to establish here before our existence is acknowledged?

Roger Tennant, Lutterworth, Leics

Even though much of the British press has been, or still is, owned by Canadians – Beaverbrook, Thomson, Black

– Canada is ignored, I have concluded, because it is the only important member of the Commonwealth that does not play Test cricket.

Lionel Loshak, Ashburton, Devon

Like other countries such as New Zealand, Portugal and Wales, Canada suffers from 'smaller neighbour syndrome'. As the pro-Canadian writer Margaret Atwood put it: 'If the national mental illness of the United States is megalomania, that of Canada is paranoid schizophrenia.' Such pointed barbs are a small price to pay for relative stability.

Gerard Mackay, Nesscliffe, Shrops

How does a country called by its inhabitants Shqiptari come to be known to the rest of the world as Albania?

The name Albania is believed to be derived from the Albanoi, an Illyrian tribe that lived in what is today central Albania, from the second century BC. Since the sixteenth century, however, Albanians themselves have called their language Shqipe, their country Shqiperia and themselves Shqiptare. Albanian scholars believe that these names are derived from the word *shqiptoj*, meaning 'to speak intelligibly'. To an Albanian, someone speaking *shqipe* would be intelligible! (Source: *Albania*, W. Bland, Cleo Press, 1988.)

Brian Palmer, St Albans, Herts

In most Italian towns there is a street called Via Venti Settembre. Why is 20 September such an important date in Italy?

The united Kingdom of Italy was proclaimed in 1861. In 1865, Venice and the Veneto were added. But the Pope clung on to what remained of the Papal States in the area immediately around Rome, known as the Patrimony of St Peter. This was defended by units of the French army at the wish of Napoleon III. At the outbreak of the Franco–Prussian war in 1870, this French garrison was withdrawn and the Italian army moved in, occupying all Rome except for the Vatican and making it possible for Rome to become the capital of Italy, as had been prom- ised. Therefore, 20 September 1870, when Italian troops entered Rome, was regarded as the culminating moment of the Italian *risorgimento* – the moment when the struc- ture of the united state was complete.

Colin Pilkington, Ormskirk, Lancs

Which country has the easiest driving test?

The small Greek island of Symi, near Rhodes, has a test

that consists of driving from the clocktower along the straight harbour road to the town square, a distance of some five hundred metres, turning the car round and driving back. One candidate has managed to fail nine times – the last time for stopping mid-test to chat with a passing relative.

Steve Pinder, London SE23

One could argue that the test in Saudi Arabia is the toughest in the world. Women are automatically banned from driving, and once you've failed the sex test there's little chance of passing on subsequent occasions.

Glyn Ford, Mossley, Lancs

According to the *Guinness Book of Records*, the driving test in Egypt used to consist of merely demonstrating the ability to drive a few metres forward and in reverse. It was made more difficult by the introduction into the test of requiring candidates to reverse between two cones. However, after 'severe cone attrition', these were replaced with two white lines.

Matthew Seward, London SW19

Argentina. In Buenos Aires you take the test on the local amusement park's 'bumper cars'. If you can crash into at least a dozen cars in the allotted time and walk away with a smile you can drive here!

Rich Coleman, San Isidro, Buenos Aires

Here in Honduras a driver's licence costs less than US$7 and takes fifteen minutes to issue. No driving test is involved. A voluntary written test of twenty questions earns you a $2 rebate. This, coupled with a total absence of traffic police, results in a driving culture that is best left to your imagination.

The official minimum age for a licence is eighteen. In practice, children of twelve or fourteen are to be found driving their parents and friends around, and most of them carry an official driver's licence.

Ian Cherrett, Santa Rosa de Copan, Honduras

My New Zealand driving test consisted of a fifteen-minute drive around the block while chatting to the cop about the All Blacks. Half-way through, and after no manoeuvres or even right turns, he said I had passed and we drove back. Incidentally, New Zealand has an appalling road safety record.

Martin Wilkinson, Devonport, Auckland

In South Dakota (in the 1950s), the day I turned fifteen I walked to the county courthouse, paid fifty cents, signed a declaration that I was not blind, and received my full drivers' permit.

Tibor Pollerman, Schrollbach, Germany

Where was the first banana republic, and who named it so?

A banana republic is a politically unstable country, with an economy dependent on one or two products, such as bananas. Furthermore, this sector is dominated by one or two companies, usually foreign–owned. The classic banana republic is Honduras, which was, from the 1880s, dominated by the American-owned United Fruit and Standard Fruit companies, whose banana exports provided the republic's foreign earnings. One reluctant American expatriate in Honduras was O. Henry, the short-story writer, fleeing from the law. He spent a year there, during which time he coined the phrase 'banana republic'. However, Honduras was not the original republic to grow bananas, which had been introduced to the Canaries and West Indies many years before.

R. L. Vickers, Crewe, Cheshire

The term is bit of a misnomer, as two of the so-called banana republics, Nicaragua and El Salvador, produce very few, if any, bananas.

Siobhan Kenny, Glasgow

NATURAL PLACES

Having experienced 52 ˚C in a dry and windy Death Valley, it doesn't feel as hot as even 30 ˚C in a humid, still-aired Singapore. So what is the hottest place on earth, not in the sense of temperature, but the combination of conditions that make it feel the hottest?

Port Sudan on the Red Sea must be a contender. The first year I lived there, the temperature rose over 50 ˚C before 9 a.m. one May morning, and for the next fourteen weeks it was between 50 ˚C and 55 ˚C every day. At night it never dropped below 42 ˚C. Despite being on the edge of a desert, because it is on the coast it is extremely humid.

In consequence, sweating does nothing to cool you down, as that depends on evaporation, which is minimal when the ambient humidity is very great and there is little wind, especially inside an office. Therefore you sweat incessantly as your body tries in vain to cool you down.

Sometimes I used to drink a litre an hour throughout the day but rarely passed water as I lost most of it through my skin.

Maurice Herson, Oxford

When I first worked in the British Council, air conditioners were almost unknown. We received, therefore, a 'hardship allowance' based on the heat and humidity of our place of posting. I believe there was a 'scale of beastliness', probably borrowed from the Foreign Office. Two of the worst, I remember, were Madras and Saigon, though I loved my Madras posting. Far hotter and less comfortable, because we had no electricity, was Juba in Southern Sudan, where even our candles wilted.

William Wood, Etchingham, East Sussex

The hottest and most humid place on earth is my bathroom after my teenage daughter has had a particularly prolonged shower.

Paul Cassidy, Huddersfield

Why are some beaches pebbly and others sandy?

Beaches consist of local materials worn from eroding cliffs or brought to the coast by rivers. So cliffs below a volcano often consist of grey or black sand, while those at Budleigh Salterton, for instance, are mainly tough, rounded pebbles from local pebble beds.

However, in most places a mixture of materials is present, as along the eroding cliffs of Norfolk or Holderness. In these cases, local contrasts between sand beaches and shingle beaches are linked to the level of wave energy reaching the coast, coarser materials indicating higher energies that can remove the finer sediment. This is emphasized by the sheltered environments of inlets and estuaries where salt marshes fronted by mudflats result from the low wave energies involved.

The relative ease with which the waves that run up the beach can percolate into the beach (rather than flow back down it) also varies with the coarseness of the beach material, and is in turn linked to the gradient (and thus inter-tidal width) of the beach. As a result, shingle beaches are steep and narrow and those with the finest sand (e.g. Rhossili Bay in south Wales) are the flattest and widest.

Keith Clayton, Norwich

How big is the sky? That is, how many square miles of it can we see, on average?

It is now generally accepted that, despite appearances,

there is no solid blue lid covering the Earth, and when there are no clouds, we can see objects millions of light years away, provided they are bright enough. The only limitation is therefore the age of the universe, currently thought to be about fifteen billion years. The universe is therefore not old enough for us to see any object further away than fifteen billion light years (about 1,024 miles), so everything we can possibly see is located within a hemisphere of that radius. The area of a hemisphere is given by $2 \times \text{pi} \times$ the square of its radius, so the area of the surface of the celestial orb is approximately $6 \times 1,048$ (six trillion, trillion, trillion, trillion) square miles.

Tim Lidbetter, Kingston

I don't think we have one. We just have a covering of impenetrable grey cloud. I think I saw it from the window of an aircraft once, but it could have been one of those clever flat-screen displays they use. It was the same colour as the video screen, and just as diverting.

David Brown, Dublin

I was dismayed to read the rather literal-minded responses to the question. Tim Lidbetter's suggestion that we see objects millions of miles away, although correct from the view of science, perpetuates the myth of scientific objectivity (the idea that human beings are somehow able to adopt the position of some quasi-divine geometer).

As a human being, my perception always operates from, and in relation to, myself. Thus, when I stand on the earth, the sky appears to vault overhead from the horizon. These concepts of sky and horizon are not accessible to scientific measurement. However, that does not make them any less an existent phenomenon. There are many things in the world that will forever elude scientific method. Fortunately, there are other 'meters' that can measure such things, such as the iambs of poetry and the rhythms of music.

Additionally, since I possess an imagination, I would reckon that here in Colchester (where we have very big skies), I can see about 1,000 square miles which are filled with frisky clouds of many exciting shapes!

Christopher Townson, Colchester, Essex

Any child will show you that it's a blue strip about one inch deep along the top of their drawing.

Margaret Pracy, Brighton

What would happen if polar bears were introduced in the Antarctic?

They would probably start eating the penguins. This is not (entirely) as silly a response as it sounds – many species of life native to particular islands or continents have been endangered or made extinct by foreign species introduced by man – consider the effect on the kiwi of the introduction of cats and dogs into New Zealand.

Andy Holyer, Lewes, East Sussex

Natural selection would see the evolution of a sub-species of polar bear with an opposable digit on one of its front paws. These 'new' polar bears would enjoy a competitive advantage: the ability to unwrap the Penguins.

With profound apologies,

Keith Davidson, Edinburgh

David Attenborough would get another series.

Peter Smith, Crewe, Cheshire

They would become bipolarized.

Tom Crow, Hillingdon, Middx

How can I ensure that there are no baby frogs on my lawn before I mow it? The grass is already very long, making it even more difficult to spot them.

Buy and release a grass snake, which will eat the frogs, even baby ones. Then you can mow the grass with a clear conscience.

Phil Cohen, Sydney, Australia

I'd like to give my remains the best possible chance of becoming fossilized. What form of burial should I choose?

In, or on, a lake bed or mud bank should do it. Chucking yourself in a glacier might do the job for a few decades, but try and pick one that will last that long.

Peter Nightingale, Reading

You could try being buried in a peat bog. A number of bodies have been preserved this way in the UK, Scandinavia and Ireland.

Julian Scott, Greystones, Co Wicklow, Ireland

You could try burial in asphalt, which naturally occurs as residue left on the surface of the ground as the lighter elements of crude oil (such as kerosene) evaporate into the atmosphere. (Asphalt is also produced as a byproduct of petroleum distillation.) Convenient to central Los Angeles is the La Brea tar pit where many fossils have been unearthed, and are on display. However, any area where petroleum has been migrating to the surface, either along a faulted sedimentary zone or along steeply dipping, porous sedimentary rock layers, have such tar pits.

David Null, Claremont, California, US

After years and years of wondering, I hope that someone can tell me the difference between a bay (for example Bengal) and a gulf (for example Mexico).

Both are sections of sea surrounded on three sides by land. If the mouth is narrow it is a gulf; if the mouth is open it is a bay. This is true for Port Philip Bay, which technically stretches to Cape Otway. Though I can see why Captain Cook would have missed the narrow bit further inland. But that was before the bay was named.

Paul Lynch, Ashiyajj, Japan

What are the benefits of global warming?

Well by my calculations, it should get rid of most of London, whereas Tavistock will become a lovely beach resort and my parents' house will treble in value. Huzzah! Oh, and it keeps those pesky environmentalists off the streets.

Jonathan Merrett, Tavistock, Devon

It will make the jobs of Antarctic geologists a lot easier.

Bob O'Hara, Helsinki, Finland

I often hear that the safest place to be in an electric storm is in a car. Given that the tyres will be wet from the heavy rain, is this good advice?

Yes, being inside a car during a lightning strike is a very safe place to be. The car is in effect a Faraday Box, a device that conducts electricity around the contents of the box without harming them. What happens if you are sitting in a Reliant Robin has yet to be scientifically demonstrated.

Richard Avery, Seville, Spain

Is it theoretically possible to create a telescope that will allow us to see the big bang?

In the only sense that the Big Bang could be seen – that is, by detecting the residual radiation that pervades the universe – you probably have one. The static displayed on an untuned television is this radiation, which the expansion of the universe has cooled from the heat of the first few seconds.

Alex Swanson, Milton Keynes

What is the longest sheer drop in the world? And exactly how far is the drop?

The film *The Abyss*, while fictional, was probably in the right area. Some ocean chasms apparently have much longer sheer drops than any of their surface counterparts, but I'm unaware of the depth of the longest. Anyone?

Glenn Oliver, Ashbourne, Devon

Challenger Deep is the deepest part of the Mariana trench, located in the western Pacific near the Philippines. The Challenger Deep is an eight-mile sheer drop.

Matt Barker, Sheffield

Dragons are cultural icons from the West (the British Isles) to the East (China/Japan) of the old world. Did we import this myth from the East centuries ago, or has it been embedded from the dawn of humanity?

The interesting thing – well interesting to me, anyway – is that dragons in the East are benign and powerful forces of nature, whereas dragons in the West are generally malevolent.

Michael Torbe, Coventry

According to Jungian psychology, dragons are an archetypal feature of our collective unconscious. They also occur in Aztec and other mythologies. However, other people have pointed out that humans have fertile imaginations and could come up with similar myths – Chinese dragons can't fly like European ones, I believe.

John Ramsey, London

Some friends of mine in Goa are plagued by monkeys. Dozens of hefty langurs conduct daily jumping matches on their roof, destroying up to 1,000 tiles annually. Friends suggested a coating of cheetah droppings – not an easy proposition. Does anyone have a better suggestion, barring death traps? (The monkey god Hanuman is venerated by Hindus.)

Get a thatched roof.

Kirsten Frederiksen, Birmingham

A friend in Kenya was plagued with monkeys on his shamba. He hollowed out some oranges, filled them with chillies and tossed them around the plot. He said it worked.

Brenda Houghton, Hampton Wick, Surrey

The simplest way without harming either the monkeys or humans would be to build a play area where the monkeys could conduct their jumping exercises, entertaining themselves and human spectators.

Harish, Chadni and Rikesh Shah, London N4

Is there any truth in the virility test for Eskimo priests who, standing naked on the ice, had to dry fourteen damp towels with the heat of their body?

I don't know about Eskimos, but Alexandra David-Neel, in her book *With Mystics And Magicians In Tibet* (Penguin, 1936) describes the practice of *tumo* or *gtumo* among Tibetan monks, which allows them to survive the winters in the hills above the snowline. This *tumo* is heat produced by the individual in a state of trance. After training, *tumo* students sit cross-legged by a frozen lake, and sheets are dipped in water and wrapped around the body. As soon as a sheet is dry, it is re-dipped and placed back to be dried once more. At least three sheets have to be dried, and stories of forty sheets in a night have been heard. Those who pass the test are called *respas* and from then on go naked or wear a single cotton garment all year round.

A. C. M. Russell, Tweedmouth, Berwick-upon-Tweed

How can I get rid of the grey squirrels in our garden without harming other animals?

Use a £30 squirrel trap available from many UK suppliers, found by doing an internet search. Use bait, disguise the trap with foliage, constrain its movement a little, alter its position occasionally, and many squirrels will be caught. The squirrels must be killed otherwise there is no point in trapping. A powerful air rifle will do this in one shot, but a lesser air rifle won't; a squirrel has a tough resilient hide. A cheaper method is to drown it in a water butt by simply immersing the trap. An immersed squirrel loses motivation in fifteen seconds. Place the bodies on your local fox trail from where they will rapidly disappear. My trap occasionally takes rats (an immersed rat loses motivation in sixty seconds), pigeons and hedgehogs (release these).

A squirrel's territory may extend over four miles, so you will be depleting the population over that range, and not just in your garden. You may therefore have to trap conscientiously for some time before noticing any effect. Keep records of your catch and if possible keep regular records of squirrel sightings in your local park. I have killed sixty grey squirrels in the past six months in a suburb of Manchester and only now does the local population seem noticeably depleted.

John Watson, Manchester

Could the rat- and squirrel-trapping John Watson confirm that his letter was written in the spirit of Jonathan Swift rather than Thomas Harris? Please?

Marian McDonagh, Mountbellew, Co Galway, Ireland

Why on earth would anyone want to kill squirrels? They might steal bird food now and again, but if that really riles you, then get a squirrel-proof bird feeder. I also live in a suburb of Manchester, and I really hope that John Watson isn't living near me and killing off the squirrels that give me so much pleasure. Let's face it, in Manchester you're grateful for any wildlife you can get.

Emilene White, Manchester

The RSPCA would always prefer that alternatives to killing squirrels are found. For example, your reader could try deterring squirrels from living in the garden in the first place.

Grey squirrels, like other wildlife, are attracted to areas where they can find food and shelter. To discourage them, block possible access points to buildings and try to reduce the amount of food available. For example, if you leave food out for the birds, use squirrel-resistant feeders rather than putting out loose food. When planting bulbs, cover them with wire mesh, deterring squirrels from digging them up.

The killing of grey squirrels should only be contemplated if there is a serious problem and alternative means have been ineffective or impractical. In this case, control should be carried out legally, be precisely targeted and carried out only by the most humane method. However, it is unlikely to be a long-term solution as their biology is such that others may quickly replace any squirrels removed from a garden.

Grey squirrels can be legally caught and killed by a variety of methods including live-catch cage traps, approved spring traps or a specific rodenticide poison that is only approved for use against grey squirrels by a local authority or professional operator. However, such methods may not be legal in areas where red squirrels could also be at risk. If a live-catch trap is used, it must be checked several times a day and any captured grey squirrels should be killed humanely. It is an offence if any unnecessary suffering is caused to captured animals.

If your reader decides to proceed with the control of grey squirrels, we suggest he contacts a reputable pest control contractor. An RSPCA information sheet is available from www.rspca.org.uk

Sarah Kennell, scientific officer, RSPCA

I hope the RSPCA tracks down Mr Watson and immerses him in a water butt until he has 'lost motivation'.

Charmian Hayes, Feltham, Middx

There is, of course, the ecclesiastical solution. I did hear of a rector who had tried various conventional methods to rid himself of the grey squirrels that were damaging his garden. In desperation he rounded them up, took them to the church and with great ceremony baptized each one; he never saw them again.

Mike Rowe, Offham, Kent

I see no reason to kill any animal simply because it is regarded as an inconvenience. However, I like to keep squirrels out of the garden when they are breeding and when the plums are ripening. For the rest of the year I'm prepared to let them entertain me with their energy and talents.

I catch the squirrels in a humane cage-type trap, using broken digestive biscuits as bait. The trap is pinned to the ground, uncamouflaged, on the lawn and the squirrels soon queue up to investigate and work out how to get the bait. Immediately after the trap is sprung, I cover the cage with a large towel to calm the squirrel and then release it in a woodland area about two-and-a-half miles away. Assuming an average of one squirrel trapped per day, it takes about ten to fourteen days to achieve a squirrel-free garden and about two months before replacements begin to appear.

I have walked through the woods where I release the squirrels for years. Their population appears to control itself, building from an average level over one or two years to a year when the population is very high (and obviously becoming unsustainable), followed by a year in which a squirrel is hard to find. This suggests to me that, as well as being barbarous, killing the many squirrels I have trapped over the years would have been ineffective as a means of controlling their numbers.

John Dann, Sutton Coldfield, West Mids

I respond to the replies to my letter about the grey squirrel. The case against the grey squirrel is robust and comprehensive. It lives at five times the population density of the red squirrel, consumes up to ten times more bio-mass than the red squirrel, and carries a virus to which it is itself immune, but the red squirrel is not.

It follows that the grey is detrimental to the promotion of diverse flora and fauna. In particular, it is continuously reducing the territory of the red squirrel, it is destructive of bird breeding activity, of tree growth and of garden and horticultural activity.

By wiping out the alien grey, we allow the less demanding and native red to repopulate, and at the same time remove a hindrance to bird breeding, tree growth and horticulture. Without intervention, the grey looks set to wipe out the native red over much of Europe. For an informed view, visit www.europeansquirrelinitiative.org.

John Watson, Manchester

Emilene White asks, 'Why on earth would anyone want to kill squirrels?'and until eighteen months ago I would have agreed with her.

During the autumn, the squirrels look for somewhere warm to have babies, and a few families chose our roof space. For three months, I listened to them partying and dancing in our loft, before finally going up to take a look. The damage had to be seen to be believed. Roofing felt was destroyed; daylight was visible through the eaves where they had gnawed access holes; bits of nesting – cardboard and fabric – were chewed and strewn everywhere, along with sawdust from eating through the rafters. They had even started to chew through the electrical wires.

The council said there would be no use repairing the damaged roof and preventing access without destroying the squirrels, because they would just return and start again. The council regards squirrels as vermin, and provided poison to kill them. The squirrels ate the poisoned food, and continued to thrive! Finally, we did manage to destroy them, and the repair of the roof, and measures to prevent future entry, cost us more than £2,000.

I now view the cute little animals in a whole new light!

Heather Toyne, Bristol

John Watson needs an Asbo – All Squirrels Bugger Off.

Harold Mozley, York

I think you now need this, an ancient Berkshire recipe no longer used since they moved us into Oxon – the squirrels aren't the same here (and only for those who do not use rodenticides, of course).

Skin and clean two squirrels. Soak in salted water with vinegar, changing several times. Dry, roll in seasoned flour. Fry in bacon fat until golden. Put in a greased pie dish with two cups of cider or beer, crushed fruit, a sliced onion, herbs. Cook slowly for two hours on hob or in oven. Then cover with pastry and cook for twenty minutes in a hot oven.

Lesley Lovell, Abingdon, Oxon

How do they measure the height of waves at sea? Does it all come down to the crude estimate of the sea-tossed mariner?

Willard Bascom, an eminent oceanographic engineer, describes how it is done in his book *Waves and Beaches*, published by Doubleday. A ship called *Ramapo*, 478 ft long, sailing from Manila to San Diego in February 1933, encountered mountainous seas. Looking astern from the bridge, the stern being in the trough of a wave, the crest of a wave was lined up with the crow's-nest. Simple geometry worked out the height from crest to trough at 112 ft, even allowing 6 ft for the height of the observer.

W Collinson, Belmont, Durham City

The reply to my question about measuring waves suggests it can be done by 'simple geometry'. If only.

The method described would work only if (a) the ship's deck were absolutely level at the moment of measurement (at the height of a gale!) or (b) the heights of the ship's stern, the observer and the crow's-nest above the water at the same moment were all known, together with (c) the measurer's distance from the foot of the mast, and, most importantly (and impossibly), (d) the exact horizontal distance of the ship from the peak of the wave being measured. Come off it!

Jack Sully, Cardiff

The estimation is rarely crude, and I doubt any mariner would ever describe himself as 'sea-tossed'.

I have had the privilege of working in the Southern Ocean for much of the past seven years, following considerable worldwide experience.

For smaller waves, the method I and some of my colleagues adopt is 'mentally transferring' a nearby familiar object of known height (e.g. a man or shipping container on deck) to the sea-surface in the trough of a wave and comparing. This gives surprisingly good results up to around 4–5 m (13–16 ft).

Beyond that, the bow and foremast of a modern merchant vessel then provide further known benchmarks within the range of 5–30 m (16–100 ft) above sea level (depending on the size of vessel). The 'final benchmark' is the vessel's bridge. The mariner is always acutely aware of his 'height of eye' above sea level (this is necessary for, among other things, determining visible range and sextant calculations). Consequently, once the crest of a wave reaches eye level, it passes another generally accurate mark.

This may sound crude, but scientific investigations have shown that experienced mariners can be accurate to within 1–2 m. Shortwave radar observations from satellites are now also able to measure the mean height of waves within a given weather system (www.ocean-weather.com has good daily charts for the world's oceans).

Within a storm system, the waves have their own complex harmonic cycle. It is normally shortly after a novice remarks, 'It seems to be getting better!' that a couple of monsters come along to instruct them to the contrary.

My own 'personal best' was in the order of 18 m (60 ft), observed from a vessel with a bridge just 9 m (30 ft) above sea level . . . I had to press my nose up against the window in order to see the crest, which was an interesting sensation!

Capt. Paul Heslop, Southsea, Hants

Given that space is infinite and we are the only inhabitants of the universe, why don't we dump toxic and nuclear waste into space?

This has been seriously assessed as a way of disposing of nuclear waste (particularly as some nuclear waste will take thousands of years to become safe) but has never really been considered for toxic waste. Most of the latter can be stored easily and its components may be processed and recycled, so space disposal would be unnecessary and extremely expensive.

For nuclear waste, disposal into space is more feasible but has been discounted on numerous occasions on the basis that should anything go wrong, the consequences could be catastrophic! A significant proportion of space launches end in disaster (often quite spectacularly so), and the prospect of a shuttle exploding, spreading large amounts of highly dangerous radioactive waste over a large area, does not bear thinking about.

Most nuclear waste is also incredibly heavy, and as the weight allowances for shuttles are very limited, it would take hundreds or even thousands of launches before a significant proportion of the world's nuclear waste could be jettisoned – increasing the chances of an accident. These shuttles would also need enough speed not just to reach an orbiting height but to completely escape Earth's gravity and, preferably, leave our solar system. So until the technology is almost 100 per cent safe, the benefits of disposing of nuclear waste into space will always be out-weighed by the risks.

Having said this, there have been plans to use nuclear

fuel as a long-lasting energy source for spacecraft travelling very long distances, as this fuel offers the distinct
advantage of having very low weight and bulk for the
amount of energy produced. Such missions may be necessary for testing the questioner's hypothesis that we are
the only inhabitants of the universe.

Matthew King, Lancaster

Many people protested at the 1997 launch of the
Cassini–Huygens mission to Saturn, as the probe carried
several kilograms of radioactive material. Even if the
launcher did explode, the radioactive material was sealed
in a blast-proof container, which should theoretically prevent its release, but there still remains an element of risk.

Adrian Hon, Kirby, Wirral

We cannot send our waste into space because there is
a treaty from the sixties on 'Principles Governing the
Activities of States in the Exploration and Use of Outer
Space, Including the Moon and Other Celestial Bodies'. It
was set up to prevent any state claiming it owned bits of
space, etc., and means that we cannot stick nuclear
weapons (or 'other weapons of mass destruction') up
there, and that states are responsible for anything they put
there.

Rachael Lorna Johnstone, University of Toronto, Canada

Whatever became of the Flat Earth Society?

My maths teacher once told my class that he was the last remaining member of the Flat Earth Society, after a successful voyage by all the other members to find the edge of the earth.

Timothy Dale, Byker, Tyneside

There are a few Flat Earth societies still operating in various parts of the world, for example in California and in India, but the original Flat Earth Society launched here in England effectively ceased to function in the mid-seventies, after the death of Sam Shenton, its longtime mainspring and advocate. There are still Flat Earth believers in this country, but to the best of my knowledge they are without an organization to help them publicize their beliefs. Through the good offices of Ellis Hillman, a councillor of the defunct Greater London Council, the Science Fiction Foundation obtained from Mrs Shenton her late husband's literary effects. The collection is available for viewing and research to any bona fide inquirer.

Charles Barren, past-chairman,
The Science Fiction Foundation, Gravesend, Kent

Following the death of Mr Shenton in 1962, Patrick Moore, the astronomer, strongly argued against dissolving the society. It is now essentially a society for challenging 'scientific orthodoxy' in the style of its late Victorian and Edwardian predecessors, the Zatetic Society and the London Dialectical Society. Although the society is subterranean and somewhat elusive, it has managed to deliver lectures at various universities. Perhaps its most notable success was its intervention at the Oxford University Scientific Society where a motion that 'This house believes that the earth is flat' was carried unanimously.

Ellis Hillman, Hendon, London NW4

The Flat Earth Society lives on, growing in influence and eccentricity since its change of name. It is now known as the Adam Smith Institute.

John Nicholls, Cranfield, Beds

As an atheist, I would rather not be buried on consecrated ground. Is there any law to stop me being buried in my garden or in a favourite piece of downland?

Surely an atheist would regard consecrated ground as no different from any other ground?

Robert Keys, Sturminster Newton, Dorset

To avoid being buried on consecrated ground, one need only ensure that there is a secular funeral. Any subsequent burial will certainly be in a local authority cemetery, which will not be consecrated. Only churchyards are consecrated and even then many extensions to churchyards are unconsecrated (mainly because of legal complications). It is perfectly possible to be buried in your own garden, as long as you have the permission of the local authority environmental health officer. There may be problems, as registered cemeteries have to be at least 100 yards from the walls of the nearest dwelling. However, Tony Walter records in his book *Funerals and How to Improve Them* (Hodder & Stoughton, 1990) that the owner of a medieval manor house got permission to be interred in the house's chapel, so all things are possible. Also bear in mind that after death your body is the property of your next of kin; and, no matter what your wishes, it is they who have the right of disposal.

(Rev Dr) Mike Parsons,
St Augustine's Vicarage, Derby

Why, when, where and by whom was it decreed that there should be 360 degrees of arc in a complete circle?

It was during the reign of Nebuchadnezzar (605–562 BC) in the Chaldean dynasty in Babylon that the circle was divided into 360 degrees. This was because the Chaldeans had calculated by observation and inference that a complete year numbered 360 days.

Gadfan Morris, Redhill, Surrey

About 4,000 years ago, the basis of angular measure for the mathematicians of Babylon was the angle at each of the corners of an equilateral triangle. They did not have decimal fractions and thus found it difficult to deal with remainders when doing division. So they agreed to divide the corner of an equilateral triangle into 60 degrees, because 60 could be divided by 2, 3, 4, 5 and 6 without remainder. Each degree was divided into 60 minutes and each minute into 60 seconds. If the angles at the corners of six equilateral triangles are placed together they form the angle formed by a complete circle. It is for this reason that there are 6 times 60 degrees of arc in the complete circle.

Steve Bolter, Braintree College, Essex

Why does the surface above an underground nuclear test sink, to form a crater, without any material appearing to be blown out of the hole? Air-to-ground filming of such tests appears to show that an implosion, rather than explosion, takes place. What has happened to the missing soil?

Underground testing of atomic bombs contains the explosion and radiation. For this reason the depth to which the bomb is buried varies from 500–600 ft to 2,000–3,000 ft, depending on the size of the bomb. When the bomb is detonated, the temperature of the blast is around 100 million °C and the pressure many millions of atmospheres. This has the effect of melting the surrounding rock and blowing it up into a huge underground bubble several hundred feet in diameter.

Shortly after the explosion, the temperature and pressure drop, leaving a void into which the overlying rock collapses. This is manifested on the surface as a crater.

Chris Waller, Yate, Bristol

A recent article on climate and weather in the *Fortean Times* mentions that Eskimos visited Scotland during the 'little ice age' of the mid-eighteenth century. Is this true?

In Aberdeen there are two kayaks in the anthropological museum of Marischal College. In an exhibition there, a few years ago, several accounts of Eskimo visits to Scotland were recounted. During the late seventeenth and early eighteenth century there were several records of strange men in canoes seen fishing off the Scottish coast. They were called 'Finmen' in the belief that they came from Finland. Around 1730 an Eskimo kayaker came ashore near Aberdeen but died soon after, and his is one of the canoes now in the museum. A century later an Eskimo named Enoolooapik was brought from Labrador to Aberdeen aboard the ship *Neptune*. He stayed for about a year, becoming a popular figure around town and occasionally giving kayaking demonstrations on the River Dee.

(Dr) Warren L. Kovach, Pentraeth, Anglesey

I have read that at sunset in the tropics, as the sun passes beneath the horizon, a 'green flash' is seen. Is this a real phenomenon, and when and where might it be seen?

The green flash is caused by the earth's atmosphere bending the sun's rays so that, towards sunset, the apparent position of the sun is some two degrees higher than its real position. Short wavelength light at the blue/green end of the spectrum is bent more than long wavelength light at the red end. This means that there are separate overlapping images of the sun with blue/green at the top and red at the bottom.

When the sun sets, the blue/green fringe is the last to sink below the horizon and, no longer swamped by light from the main disc of the sun, is briefly visible.

Observations of the green flash are not confined to the tropics and can, on occasion, be seen almost anywhere with a clear horizon when atmospheric conditions are right. If the disc of the setting sun appears very reddened, the green flash is unlikely to be seen because most of the short wavelength blue/green light has been scattered out by atmospheric particles.

Philip G. Griffiths, consultant ophthalmologist,
Newcastle general hospital

The flash has a number of slightly variant forms – it may be a thin band just above the sun's disc and it may be blue or violet or even changing. It can even occur before the sun starts to set and there may be a 'red flash' below the sun.

The green flash was fist popularized by an 1882 novel of Jules Verne, *Le Rayon Vert*, about a search for it. Though described by Lord Kelvin in a letter to *Nature* in 1899, it was long generally believed to be some sort of visual illusion. Attempts to photograph it with an ordinary camera are futile as the flash is too small to register on the film. It was not until 1954 that colour photographs were obtained using specially adapted telescopes at the Vatican Observatory at Castel Gandolfo.

David Singmaster, London SW4

The 'green flash' is much sought on the north coast of

Cornwall. I have seen it twice – once from Newquay and, more recently, returning from an evening walk to Stepper Point, near Padstow.

Keith Richards, London N12

Rock samples were brought back from the Moon by the Apollo space missions in the late sixties and early seventies. Were they similar to rocks found on Earth, or were they totally different? And are any minerals on the Moon worth exploiting?

Moon rocks are all volcanic and are comparable with similar rocks on Earth, although there are slight but significant chemical differences, because the Moon is a fossil world, unchanged for the past 3,800,000,000 years. This is the age of the youngest moon rocks, older than any existing earth rocks and therefore belonging to an early period of planetary evolution. On Earth, rocks of this period have long ago been recycled by the processes of plate tectonics and weathering. Because of its smaller size, the Moon lacks these, having frozen into a static world nearly 4,000,000,000 years ago, while the larger Earth has continued to sustain both internal and surface activity.

David Land, Edinburgh

In an article in *Scientific American* for July 1994, Professor G. Jeffrey Taylor, who chairs the committee that advises Nasa on its missions, describes the outcome of studying the 382 kilograms of rock samples collected from the Moon twenty-five years ago. This analysis supported the view that the Moon originated from a glancing collision between Earth and another protoplanet 4,500,000,000 years ago.

The impact may be one of the factors that made Earth habitable, by speeding up its rotation time from perhaps a year to a day. The heat generated left the Moon covered with sea of molten rock and devoid of water. A more systematic collection covering more of the Moon's surface could test the theory that the evolution of life on Earth has been driven by mass extinctions, of 90 per cent or more of species and individuals living at the time, caused by impacts from smaller objects at intervals of tens of millions of years. Professor Taylor concludes: 'Only by continuing the legacy of Apollo can we hope to complete our understanding of our place in the solar system.'

(Prof.) Romaine Hervey, Wells, Somerset

What is the universe expanding into?

The simple answer is 'itself'. The universe is all there is; it has no outside. This is not the same as saying 'there is nothing outside' as that requires a boundary and the universe is boundless.

The commonest metaphor used to try to visualize this is the child's balloon. The rubber of an inflating balloon expands, every point on it gets further from every other. Yet to a two-dimensional population living on its surface, their world is not expanding into anything, but mysteriously getting bigger. Of course, with this analogy of the universe, the big bang comes at the wrong end!

Patrick O'Neill, Eastleigh, Hants

It is not a vacuum, as that is inside the universe and is traversed by electrical, magnetic and gravitational fields. So one could describe the space beyond the boundary of the universe as nothing – a lack of anything, except, perhaps, thought of conscious beings.

Matter expanding into 'nothing' at the boundary of the universe will have a negative electrical charge because this is repelled by radiation pressure and will accelerate much more than relatively heavy matter with positive charges. This produces an increasing potential gradient, and eventually immense electrical discharges form huge jets of positively charged matter, which condense to form the strings of galaxies we can now observe with our sophisticated telescopes and even binoculars. Most of the current 'mysteries' of astronomy can be explained without postulating bizarre ideas about so-called black holes and cosmic strings.

Eric Crew, Broxbourne, Herts

Whatever happened to the 'Bermuda Triangle'?

It disappeared without trace in mysterious circumstances.

Peter Sommer, London N4

The Bermuda Triangle, a vaguely defined area in the north Atlantic supposedly associated with a number of unexplained crashes, disappearances and other 'paranormal' phenomena, reached the height of its popularity during 1965–75.

Its demise followed the realization that the number of reported sinkings and other accidents was not at all exceptional for the amount of sea and air traffic that normally passes through the area. Careful analysis of individual incidents showed that logical and familiar explanations could be found for almost all of them, and that there was no more reason to search for a single cause than there would be for all the road accidents in southern England.

In what is probably the definitive book on the subject, *The Bermuda Triangle Mystery – Solved* by Lawrence David Kusche, the author concludes:

The legend of the Bermuda Triangle is a manufac-
tured mystery. It began because of careless research
and was elaborated upon and perpetuated by writers
who either purposely or unknowingly made use of
misconceptions, faulty reasoning and sensationalism.
It was repeated so many times that it began to take
on the aura of truth.

The Bermuda Triangle may no longer be with us but, for
those who need such things, psychic surgery, alien abduc-
tions, spoon-bending and corn circles seem to have proved
more than adequate substitutes.

Michael Hutton, Camberwell, London SE5

As everyone who lives and works in west London will
know, this has shifted to west London. It is now known as
the 'Southall Triangle' and is located near Hayes Bridge.
In spite of a clearly illuminated display, indicating the
time of arrival of the next bus, number 207 buses frequently disappear a minute or so before they are due.

Many will also be aware that all planes approaching or
departing from Heathrow carefully avoid this area.

Eric Parsons, Southall

**What is a continent? Is Europe a continent or just
the western part of the Asian landmass?**

Europe and Asia have been welded together for at least 300 million years. Geophysically, continents are defined by the thickness and composition of their crust, which (unlike oceanic crust) is silica rich and thick. There are seven patches of continental crust, but it makes sense to subdivide them where they are cut by tectonic plate boundaries, because the fragments are in relative motion. This makes fourteen continents in all: Jan Mayen, the Rockall Plateau, the Agulhas Plateau (south of South Africa), the Seychelles, New Zealand, Antarctica, South America, Central America, North America (including a large chunk of Siberia), Eurasia, Australia, India, Arabia and Africa.

Graham Cogley, professor of geography,
Trent University, Peterborough, Canada

Continents are pieces of physical geography that we think have some cultural unity. The Greeks began this by calling the different shores of the Mediterranean (Mid-Earth Sea), Europe, Asia and Africa. But they settled all three and Alexander the Great's conquests began a unification completed by the Romans, whose empire encircled Mare Nostrum (Our Sea). Europe re-emerged when the Islamic conquests stopped at the Mediterranean, which became a moat around Christendom.

Only from the sixteenth century onwards did Europeans impose the idea of continents on the world.

Missionary-educated 'Asians' and 'Africans' learned to accept these definitions. Everywhere except Antarctica is just a 'peninsula of Asia' in strict physical terms.

John Newson, Birmingham

What is the geological explanation for the red rock stacks in Monument Valley, Arizona?

The guide booklet produced by the Navajo Nation Parks & Recreation Dept gives the following explanation:

> For hundreds of millions of years, materials that eroded from the early Rocky Mountains deposited layer upon layer of sediments which cemented over the years into rock: sandstone and limestone. Then, a slow and gentle uplift, generated by ceaseless pressure from below the surface, elevated these horizontal strata quite uniformly 1–3 miles above sea level. What was once a basin became a plateau. Natural forces (wind and water) spent the last 50 million years cutting into and peeling away at the surface of the plateau. The simple wearing down of alternate layers of soft and hard rock slowly revealed the natural wonders of Monument Valley today.

Robert Davidson, Epsom, Surrey

What differences would there be were the Earth not to have a moon, and what would be their consequences?

Werewolves would wonder what was going on.

A. O'Reilly, Nottingham

The Earth's surface could never have been turned into a mixture of land and ocean without the Moon's tidal drag working over billions of years, and advanced life could never have appeared if our world had been all land or all water. In 1988, Dr Jerome Pearson of the Flight Dynamics Laboratory in Dayton, Ohio, pointed out that the ocean tides, directly caused by the Moon, and the emergence of tidewater zones, which alternate between flooding and drying out, probably helped life to emerge on land. Also, the huge gravitational tide of the Moon was responsible for the Earth's molten core, which has opened and closed ocean basins and separated continents, isolating gene pools and speeding up evolution. Additionally, the Moon has probably served as a partial shield against meteoric bombardment from space, further enhancing the prospects for intelligent life.

Tony Martin, Nunhead, London SE15

Tony Martin is wrong on what causes the tides. If the Moon did not exist, our tides would be almost unchanged because they are caused almost entirely by the Sun. The gravitational force between two bodies is proportional to the product of their masses, divided by the square of their separation. The Sun's mass is 27 million times greater than the Moon's, giving a gravitational force 176 times greater. The effect of the Moon is, therefore, negligible.

D. Fitzgerald, Ilkley, West Yorks

D. Fitzgerald correctly states that the Sun produces tides on the Earth. These tides, however, have less than half the magnitude of the tides produced by the Moon. It is not the strength of the gravitational pull of the Moon that matters, but the difference in the strengths of the gravitational field due to the Moon at the points on the Earth nearest to, and farthest from, the Moon. This depends on the mass of the Moon, and on the ratio of the diameter of the Earth (7,900 miles) to the distance from the Earth to the Moon (239,000 miles). The same is true in the case of the Sun. Even at 93 million miles, the gravitational field due to the Sun is much stronger than that due to the Moon, but it is changing more slowly with distance.

When the Sun and Moon are in line, their tides add up to give a large rise and fall (spring tides). When they are pulling at right angles to one another, their tides tend to cancel out (neap tides).

Jim Stacey, Thornton, Liverpool

Are there any theories as to why the Moon and Sun are exactly the right size to give us eclipses?

Total eclipses are possible because the Moon, which is 400 times smaller than the Sun, is also 400 times closer. The disc of the Moon therefore fits almost exactly over the disc of the Sun when viewed from the right location on Earth during a total eclipse. Most astronomers are quite happy to accept that this is simply a coincidence. After all, there is nothing particularly significant about a total eclipse other than the fact that it looks pretty. Is there really anything that needs explaining? Do we need to explain why a given set of six numbers comes up on the national lottery, even if they are the six we have on our ticket?

Total eclipses are in any case quite rare. Owing to the fact that the Earth–Moon and Earth–Sun distances vary significantly during the course of a year, eclipses often occur in which the Moon's disc is smaller than that of the Sun. These are called annular eclipses. The most common kind of eclipse is one in which the Moon just bites a chunk off the Sun's disc, and this doesn't require any coincidence in size or distance. What's more, the Earth–Moon separation is steadily increasing, so if we wait long enough (hundreds of millions of years), there won't be any total eclipses at all!

But even if this is a coincidence, perhaps it is not as much of a coincidence as you might think. We do not know how many other 'solar systems' there are in the universe, how many of those involve planets like Earth, or how many of those have moons, and so on. Among the other solar systems out there, there will probably be many in which the orbits and sizes are such that eclipses are never seen. But solar systems too different from our own may not have developed complex life in the way ours has, and among those with life, total eclipses are probably more common than those without. Although this doesn't 'explain' the coincidence, it does suggest that the odds against it are not as long as one might first think.

Professor Peter Coles, School of Physics and Astronomy,
University of Nottingham

It is often said that the only man-made object visible from space is the Great Wall of China. How can this be so, since, despite its obvious length, it is relatively narrow?

The Great Wall of China cannot be seen from space. However, due to dust storms a clear line is often visible from space where the dust meets the barrier of the Wall, so the astronauts can see its exact position. Major cities at night and large areas of reclaimed land such as those in the Netherlands are man-made objects that are visible from space.

Martin Lewis, Bradford, West Yorks

The world's largest building (by area of land that it covers) can be seen from space. The roof of the Chek Lap Kok airport building in Hong Kong covers well over one square kilometre.

Steve King, London W9

MYTHICAL AND
MYSTERIOUS PLACES

At at least five locations in London (all above the Northern Line) there is a circular-based building of roughly 6 m diameter and 3 m height with no obvious features, and on top of it a smaller square-based structure with thin horizontal windows. The most obvious one is at the south-east corner of Clapham Common. Does anyone know what these buildings are?

In 1940, at the height of the Blitz, Herbert Morrison announced a series of ten deep-level shelters underneath various underground stations. The shelters at St Paul's and Oval were never completed; Chancery Lane and Clapham Common were used as emergency citadels against V1 and V2 rockets; Goodge Street was used as a base for General Eisenhower whilst Stockwell became a hostel for American troops. The other four (Clapham North,

Clapham South, Camden Town and Belsize Park) were opened to the public. It was intended that the shelters would become part of a high-speed underground line after the war but this never happened. The Camden Town shelter was later used for a *Doctor Who* story and I believe Goodge Street was used to house soldiers en route to Suez. (Information taken from *London Under London* by Richard Trench and Ellis Hillman.)

Mitchell Sandler, London N2

The Clapham Common site was the original entrance to the Northern Line. As the area has slowly gentrified, the barbed-wire-covered monstrosity has become increasingly obvious and offensive. In 1997, the Cabinet Office advertised all seven for sale, stating: 'The shelters are typically made up of two parallel tunnels divided horizontally to create two levels of accommodation totalling up to 6,750 square metres per property. Access to each of the tunnels is by lift and stairs from two surface sites. They have been put on the market for a total guide price of £2,757,500.'

Ed Young, London SW4

A note in the family archives states that my grandfather 'during the Great War worked with Sir Alfred Ewing in the famous Room 40'. Famous for what?

Room 40 was the First World War precursor of Bletchley Park and, later, GCHQ. At the outbreak of war, the Royal Navy set Admiral Sir Reginald 'Blinker' Hall to work on developing communications intelligence – radio interception and codebreaking. He formed a disparate team of academics and others, who worked out of Room 40 in the Old Block at the Admiralty and broke over 20,000 German messages over the course of the conflict. Much of this was done using a number of captured diplomatic, civil and naval codebooks.

Winston Churchill, as First Lord of the Admiralty, ensured that the activities of Room 40 remained a deep secret. Phillip Knightley, in *The Second Oldest Profession* (1986), describes how the security was so tight that Admiral Jellicoe was prevented from receiving information that could have allowed a victory at Jutland in May 1916.

John O'Shea, Birmingham

Towards the end of the nineteenth century the Jezreels society/sect had a six-storey 'temple' at New Brompton in Kent. Does either the building or the group still exist?

My childhood in Gillingham was dominated by the huge gaunt shell of the Jezreel's Tower; standing on the highest point in the Medway Towns, it loomed over the whole area. It was built to be the church and headquarters of the New and Latter House of Israel, commonly known as the 'Jezreelites' after their founder James Jershom Jezreel (né James Rowland White), who formed a splinter group from a local Christian Israelite branch in 1875. He preached physical immortality for the chosen, but inconsiderately died before his grandiose tower was started in 1885. Funds ran out in 1888 and the building was left roofless. It was sold in 1905, the fittings stripped out and the height reduced from its original 120 ft. The Co-op eventually bought it and used the cellars for storage, but the tower itself never found a purpose. In 1961, Gillingham Borough Council, in an act of short-sighted vandalism, allowed the tower to be demolished. The site was supposedly for light industrial units, but only one was ever built.

Many tales circulated locally about the Jezreelites, the daftest being that they never cut their hair so that on Judgement Day they would ascend to the top of the tower and God could haul them up to Heaven by their unshorn locks. There have been two books about Jezreel and his tower: *The Sixth Trumpeter* by P. G. Rogers (OUP, 1963) and *The Jezreelites* by R. A. Baldwin (Lambourne Press, 1962).

The New and Latter House of Israel is still in existence; it advertises regualarly in alternative health magazines. The most recent address I've seen is in Hailsham, Sussex.

Geoff Ross, Hadleigh, Suffolk

Many English cathedrals, like Salisbury and Wells, have attached buildings known as Chapter Houses, often octagonal in shape. What was their original purpose? And is there any special reason for the eight-sided design?

Chapter houses were used for meetings, called chapters, to conduct the business affairs of a monastery or cathedral and to deal with matters for which the church itself would not be appropriate. Within a monastery this would also include the reading of a portion (a chapter) of the Book of the Rule, assignment of duties of the day, reading of letters and sealing of deeds and documents; accusations and confessions of transgressions against the Rule were made, and punishment pronounced.

Every monastery and cathedral had a chapter house. These were nearly always rectangular and were the most important building after the church itself. Thirty centrally planned chapter houses were constructed between 1100 and 1500; although about two-thirds were octagonal, there are circular, decagonal and even duodecagonal examples. Circular plans had become outmoded by 1200, but there seems to be no technical, theological or functional reason for preferring the octagon, although they are easier to set out and construct than, say, hexagons or decagons.

Jon Bolter, London N1

Does anyone know the original use of the pedestrian subway running from South Kensington tube station to a point near Imperial College? It seems to be only a few yards beneath the surface and is quite elaborately constructed, considering its apparent age.

The subway was originally constructed for visitors to exhibitions held on land in Kensington. The Fisheries Exhibition of 1883, the Health Exhibition of 1884, the Inventions Exhibition of 1885 and the Colonial and Indian Exhibition of 1886 drew crowds of up to 5.5 million so in 1885 the subway was opened, leading directly to the exhibition site and charging a 1d toll. The exhibition series was continued at Earl's Court after 1886, when the original site was needed for the building of Imperial College.

Sarah Todd, York

The subway was built by the Metropolitan District Railway, the forerunner of London Underground's District Line. Once the exhibitions moved to Earl's Court, the railway found itself with a white elephant and for a number of years the subway was opened only on special occasions. A 1906 proposal for an extension to Princes Gate to serve the Royal Albert Hall was not proceeded with. Toll collection having become uneconomical, the subway was opened permanently on 21 December 1908 free of charge. New exits/entrances for the Natural History and Victoria & Albert Museums were opened in 1913.

Michael Smith, Swaffham, Norfolk

In several places on the outskirts of London, I have seen white-painted posts about nine inches square and three feet high. What are they? On one face is a shield on which is painted a red cross. Below the shield is written '24 & 25 Vic' and below that 'Cap 42'.

The posts are known as City or Coal Tax posts. To cover rebuilding costs after the Great Fire of 1666, the Corporation of London was allowed to levy a charge on all coal entering London. Subsequently there were a number of acts defining the boundaries of the area for which duty was charged, until finally in 1861 the London Coal and Wine Duties Continuance Act redefined the London District as the Metropolitan Police District. Posts were set up to mark the boundary in accordance with this Act of Parliament of the 24th and 25th years of Queen Victoria's reign (chapter 42 of the Statute Book). The cast-iron posts bear the Corporation of London crest (the shield with the red cross) and the inscription mentioned:

'24 & 25 VIC CAP 42'. They were originally placed wherever a road or track crossed the boundary. Different types of marker posts were often employed beside railways, canals and rivers. The iron posts were cast by Henry Grissel at the Regents Canal Ironworks in Hoxton, central London; they are 6 ft high of which 3–4 ft is above ground. The duties continued to raise money for engineering projects in London until the formation of the London County Council and the passing of the London Coal Duties Abolition Act in 1889. (Source: *Industrial History of the Mole Valley* by Peter Tarplee.)

Alun Roberts, Leatherhead Museum of Local History, Surrey

I was recently shown some photographs taken in the sixties of shop fronts, said to be in a street 'beneath' Oxford Street in London. Could this be true? If so, can they still be visited?

'Tiles Street' was a mini arcade of shops (fashion shops, a beauty parlour, a coffee bar) situated within Tiles Club, a sixties basement discotheque on Oxford Street. The club, which was open on weekdays at lunchtime, and its clientele are documented by Tom Wolfe in 'The Noonday Underground' (*The Pump House Gang*, 1968). The club closed when its owners lost money investing in a pop festival at Woburn Abbey. In the seventies the premises became an aquarium. The site was further redeveloped (as offices, I believe) in the eighties.

Paul Sowerbutts, Highgate, London N10

When the Holy Family fled to Egypt, were they bogus asylum-seekers or economic migrants?

It depends what paper you read.

Jennifer Hall, Camberley, Surrey

Clearly, they were bogus asylum-seekers. They fled from Judaea not because of any harm Herod had already done to them, but because of a prediction – an accurate one, as it turned out – of what he was about to do. (To the best of my knowledge, prophetic dreams are not admissible in law.)

Herod's actual victims, the holy innocents, would have had a valid claim for asylum, since Herod's evil intentions towards them were beyond dispute. By that time, unfortunately, they were dead.

(Sister) Rosemary, Community of the Holy Name, Radford, Nottingham

I don't know about the Holy Family, but I recently heard a Bible reading that informed us that when Moses was in Egypt he 'lived as a resident alien'.

Elizabeth Swinbank, York

Either way, I've often wondered whether Joseph and Mary declared their son's gold, frankincense and myrrh, or were they technically tax dodgers?

K. Joyce, Lewisham, London

Why does nothing in my house work properly?

Really the question should be, why does nothing in this country work properly?

Robert Nolan, Truro, Cornwall

The simple answer is, 'because'.

Simon Gray, Newhaven, East Sussex

Try reading Robert Pirsig's *Zen and the Art of Motorcycle Maintenance*.

Laurel Farrington, Hitchin, Herts

Try paying the bills, Robert, it works every time.

Kirsten Frederiksen, Birmingham

You think that's bad? Nothing works in my bedsit.

Steven Patrick, Manchester

Why are boxing rings square?

Although boxing existed in Ancient Greece (in a particularly brutal form), and fist-fights between two opponents have been popular through the ages, it was not until the eighteenth century that it became properly established in England.

Boxers would visit towns and villages and challenge members of the public to take them on. At first, bouts were usually held outdoors. The spectators would stand in a circle around the fighters, holding a length of rope to confine the boxers in a clearly defined space, and this, being a circle, came to be known as the boxing ring.

But as the sport became more popular and numbers of spectators increased, this method became impractical. Instead, the arena was marked out by four wooden stakes, forming a square, and joined by a length of rope. But old habits die hard, and long-established names linger on. And so the arena, although technically a square, was, and still is, referred to as a 'boxing ring'.

Edward Phillips, London N5

If they were round, where would a boxer's corner be?

James Meadows, London SE19

Where did people congregate before water-coolers became ubiquitous in offices? And why did they congregate here in the first place

– surely the coffee machine would be more convenient?

Going back to the sixties, seventies and eighties, even coffee machines were not much in evidence. People congregated around photocopiers (the consequence of slow copy speeds, frequent jams and the lack of personal printers). Better still, we all went to the pub at lunchtime and even more enthusiastically as soon as possible in the late afternoon.

The informal gathering for a chat in the office space during the working day is a relatively new thing. However, some companies have deliberately designed their offices around a spacious central eating/drinking/meeting area and this seems to result in very high levels of productive social interaction and communication: not just for gossip but for business-related interchanges.

H. Robert Mann, London W8

Interestingly, 'scuttlebutt', the common American expression for water-cooler gossip, was originally a nautical term for a water barrel from which crew members could drink, probably as far back as Nelson's navy or beyond. So it seems that the practice may be at least two centuries old.

Nick Sharman, Congleton, Cheshire

About forty years ago a substantial project was launched in Alaska, with US government support. It started with a big hole, the intention being to keep digging to see what happened. It was called the Mohole experiment. What happened?

The Mohole project was an attempt to retrieve a sample of material from the earth's mantle by drilling a hole through the Earth's crust to the Mohorovicic discontinuity [the boundary between the earth's crust and mantle, across which there is a sudden change in velocity of seismic waves], or Moho. The project was proposed in 1957 by Walter Munk, a member of the National Science Foundation Earth Science Panel in the US; initial drilling was actually off the cost of Mexico rather than in Alaska.

Phase one (of three planned phases) began in earnest with a set of drillings in March and April 1961. Five holes, one of which extended 601 ft beneath the seafloor, were drilled under 11,700 ft of water. Cores obtained from the holes showed that the first layer of crust extended 557 ft and consisted of sediment that was Miocene in age. The second layer of crust was found to consist of basalt.

In 1966, Congress objected to the costs of the programme before the implementation of phase two. If successful, this exploration of the intraterrestrial frontier would have provided invaluable information on the Earth's age, makeup and internal processes. In addition, evidence drawn from the Moho could have been brought to bear on the question of continental drift, which at the time was still controversial. It was described as the 'earth sciences' answer to the space programme'.

Given the competing priority of finding vast amounts of money to put men on a lifeless rock a quarter of a million miles from Earth before the Soviets did, not to mention the cost of hardware for killing anything that moved in south-east Asia, it's entirely understandable that Munk's little project should have been abandoned.

Richard Savory, Witney, Oxon

Why are there Greek crosses carved in kerbstones in Greek Street, Soho? There are a few similar crosses in nearby Soho Square.

Greek Street was laid out in the late 1670s and early 1680s, and named after a colony of Christian Greeks from Melos sought refuge in England and became an established part of the local community. Their chapel, built 1677–80, was in Hog Lane (now Charing Cross Road), which ran parallel to the east. It was later taken over by French Huguenot immigrants (until 1822) and the site is now covered by St Martin's School of Art.

Basil Morgan, Uppingham, Rutland

Etruria (near Wolverhampton), Aspatria (Cumbria). What are the origins of such Continental-sounding placenames and how many other examples are there?

There's Strata Florida in Wales.

Bryn Jones, Welwyn Garden City, Herts

Etruria was called after Josiah Wedgwood's eighteenth-century house and pottery works, which he called Etruria after the ancient country in central Italy (now Tuscany), famous for its fine artworks, especially pottery.

Aspatria is part-Scandinavian: from *askr*, an ash-tree, plus the name Patrick, and means '(place by) St Patrick's ash-tree'. (See *Dictionary Of Place-Names* by A. Room and *Dictionary Of English Place-Names* by A. D. Mills.)

Many placenames in England are not English. Tarvin (Cheshire) is Welsh; Malpas (Cheshire and other counties) is French; Toller Porcorum (Dorset) is Celtic plus Latin, and any number of place-names in Cumbria, north-east England, Yorkshire and Wirral (Cheshire) are Scandinavian. This reflects the many contributors to the richness of the English language.

J. A. P. Dutton, Ellesmere Port, Cheshire

What is the origin of the placename 'Jacob's Well',

which appears in various parts of the north of England?

The name is attached to springs just outside the towns of Bradford, Wakefield and Guildford. It clearly derives from the well, now incorporated into a partially completed church, a mile outside ancient Shechem in Palestine. Jesus is reported in the New Testament (John 4–6) as encountering at this well a woman from a 'Samaritan' village; both being excluded from drinking at the town well – Jesus as a mainstream Jew, the woman by reason of her adultery.

The 'Samaritans' were Jews who chose Shechem for the centre of their worship (as they still do); it having been the original cultic sanctuary for the Hebrews, and particularly associated with the patriarch Jacob.

Tom Hennell, Withington, Manchester

We lived in Jacob's Wells Road in Bristol – I think the sign over the door gave the date of 1087. It was the ritual well of the Jewish community in Bristol, but when they were thrown out in the fourteenth century, the name was changed to Woodwell. I don't know when it was changed back, but a map of 1821 still shows the road as Woodwell Lane.

Theresa Graham, Mathern, Chepstow

In the Arabian Nights, why do the words 'Open sesame' open the cave door? Is it to do with sesame seed oil oiling the hinges, or does it come from an Arabic word?

This was explained in a Popeye cartoon when our hero cries, 'Open, says me' and the gates open.

Alan Brown, Wolverhampton

It is not an Arabic word, it is Anglo-Italian. Chico, on finding the door locked, wanted to force it. Harpo became agitated so Chico called, 'Open sesa-him.' No luck. Groucho, dressed in a rather fetching evening gown, wanted to try. 'Open sesa-her,' said Chico. No luck. Chico, becoming annoyed, said, 'Open sesa-them.' And then, 'Open sesa-us.' As a last resort, he cried, 'Open sesa-me.'

The custodian, getting nervous of a potential *Night at the Opera*, opened the door. He didn't want an excruciating playing of Agrarian Nights by Ripsha Corsets-Off, so he gave in.

I don't know where the Arabic thing comes into it.

Steve Tague, Morden, Surrey

Is smoking allowed in heaven?

Assuming, for the sake of argument, that the questioner

envisions heaven as a physical entity to which all right-eous souls pass after death, an extension of earthly life but without evil, then smoking would be eminently permissi-ble. All that would be excluded from this vision of heaven is that which is evil; all substances are God's creation, and cannot in themselves be good or evil, so there is tobacco in heaven, along with hemlock, cocaine, anthrax and all sorts of other nasty natural substances.

A more interesting question is whether the smoker can pass into heaven, as smoking could be interpreted as a sin: to smoke today is to be aware of the health risks and ignore them; this could be interpreted as suicide, which is a sin because all life is, as God's creation, sacred.

The question is of intent, however. If one smokes for pleasure, then even if their life ends as a result, the intent was not to kill, therefore they can pass into heaven. As a gratuitous pleasure, smoking could not be regarded as a truly Christian action, but it is nevertheless not a sin.

Once in heaven and blessed of eternal life, smoking becomes utterly harmless and therefore can undoubtedly be engaged in with abandon. I certainly expect my first words to St Peter to be: 'Got a light?'

Arthur Newman, Norwich

Only on Ash Wednesday.

John Somers, Honiton, Devon

Perhaps. But it's compulsory in the other place.

Doyle P. Cross, Dagenham Essex

This story may throw some light on the question. Or perhaps not.

A novice monk consults an older monk: 'Is it in order for me to smoke while meditating?' He is told brusquely: 'Most certainly not!' Next day he asks the abbot: 'Is it in order for me to meditate while smoking?' The abbot replies benignly: 'Certainly you may, my son.'

Tony Tantram, Bookham, Surrey

Where will it all end?

The questioner is making one explicit assumption and an implicit one, both of which are debatable. One is that it will have an end. We humans have an end, though given that matter cannot be destroyed, that is true only in a sense. However, why assume that it will end? The implicit one is that 'it' began, whereas perhaps 'it' has an eternal past just as much as an infinite future. I'll go out on a limb and say that we'll never know.

Ivor Solomons, Norwich

It'll be all right in the end. So if it isn't all right, it isn't the end yet.

Wendy Bradley, Bangor, Wales

In tears.

Aidan Sammons, Brierley Hill, Dudley

The end has already begun in the centre of the universe, as the oldest part of the universe ages and dies. The location of the end will probably be on the fringes of the universe, as stars currently being born eventually succumb to entropy and all matter is reduced to the zero energy point. This will make location as we understand it irrelevant, as there will no longer be any point of reference.

If 'When will it all end?' had been asked, the answer is much happier, as the answer is: not for a good long while.

William Spratt, York

Stop, Georgia, US (33° 28' 47N, 84° 35' 20W)

Stephen Boylan, Dublin

If the island of Sodor were a real place, how big would it have to be to sustain the transport infrastructure of Thomas the Tank Engine?

On the Rev. Awdry's map, Sodor is situated next to the Isle of Man and is considerably bigger than the latter. Therefore it is plenty big enough to sustain the Fat Controller's railway – although it's not as good as it used to be since the Conservatives privatized it.

Mark Fletcher, London

What's wrong with clouds one to eight?

They're too low. The expression 'on cloud nine' came into use shortly after the publication of the first *International Cloud Atlas* in 1896 ('the International Year of Clouds'). The atlas classified clouds by height, giving each cloud-type a number. The highest – cloud nine – was Cumulonimbus, the towering thundercloud, which can build to a height of ten miles or more. To be 'on cloud nine' was thus to be higher than anything else on earth.

Sadly, the latest edition of the *Cloud Atlas* (1995) has renumbered the cloud-types: cloud nine is now the low-flying Cumulus, while the majestic Cumulonimbus has been promoted to cloud ten.

Richard Hamblyn, author of
The Invention of Clouds, *London E17*

The origin of cloud nine is derived from Buddhism. The state of being 'Cloud nine' is the penultimate goal of Bhodisattva (enlightenment).

Cloud one is Great Perfection Brightness Cloud; cloud two, Great Compassion Brightness Cloud; cloud three, Great Wisdom Brightness Cloud; cloud four, Great Pranja Brightness Cloud; cloud five, Great Samadhi Brightness Cloud; cloud six, Great Auspicious Brightness Cloud; cloud seven, Great Good Fortune Brightness Cloud; cloud eight, Great Merit Brightness Cloud; cloud nine, Great Refuge Brightness Cloud; cloud ten, Great Praise Brightness Cloud.

(Mrs) P. White, Carnforth, Lancs

According to Guy Mitchell there's nothing wrong with cloud seven, or 'Cloud Lucky Seven' as he calls it in his song. It's the cloud 'nearest heaven' and you reach it 'when you're in love, when you're in love, when you're in love.' In fact 'your heart jumps and kicks on clouds five and six.' So they sound pretty good as well.

Terry Taylor, Bury St Edmunds, Suffolk

Why do we never hear about ghosts in churches? Is there some automatic exorcism process there?

According to *Exorcism: The Report of a Commission Convened by the Bishop of Exeter* (1972), all places – including churches – 'may be strained and influenced by a variety of causes, and frequently by more than one of them at the same time'. The majority of such 'haunts' are 'place memories', 'impersonal traces of earlier personal action, and seem to be caused either by habitual actions or by actions accompanied by violent emotion'.

On the recommendation of the commission the Archbishop of Canterbury (Donald Coggan) in 1975 issued guidelines encouraging the bishops to formulate 'appropriate policy' for their dioceses – in other words the appointment of exorcists or teams of 'deliverance ministers'. All Church of England dioceses now have clergy appointed to this task.

(Rev) Alan Walker, London NW11

When I lived at Wimborne, the then sacristan of the minster claimed to have had two paranormal experiences. One involved glimpsing a woman in 1920s clothing at the vestry door, who was nowhere to be found when he went to speak to her. On the other occasion he said he had heard footsteps of somebody running up one of the aisles when he was alone in the building.

John Saville, Duffield, Derbyshire

No. Frankly, if you where a ghost, would you want to sit around a church all day for the rest of eternity? I find one hour is already enough.

Mairead McGuirk (aged 13), London SW20

They always seem to talk about the Holy Ghost whenever I've been.

Nick Lee, London SE22

In the sixties my mother saw a whole ghostly congregation in Cirencester parish church when she was attending a service. They were dressed in very old-fashioned clothes and seemed to be following a different order of service, as they stood and knelt at different times to the real congregation. She didn't find them frightening, no one else was aware of them, and they were not aware of the real congregation.

I was interested to read the Rev. Walker's statement that such hauntings may be caused by traces resulting from habitual actions or strong emotions, as my mother had a number of such paranormal experiences during her lifetime and thought they may have been caused by just this sort of 'stone tape' process, whereby a location can act as a mechanism to record and replay certain events when conditions are right.

Barbara Jennings, London SW17

We don't hear about ghosts in churches because ghosts haunt the place where they died, and very few people die on hallowed ground.

Chris Rogers, Edgware, Middx

Cursory examination of the welter of books on folklore or hauntings in the UK shows that in some areas almost every church seems to have a permanent ghostly resident.

The most famous haunting of the 1930s was Borley Rectory on the Essex/Suffolk border. Nearby Langenhoe church was described by veteran ghost-hunter Peter Underwood as 'certainly haunted'.

In fact, given the effect of religion upon the history of the British Isles (albeit an occasionally violent effect), it is not surprising that so many places of worship are allegedly haunted. Indeed, it sometimes appears that a large proportion of the 'ghosts' are seen in churches and, thanks to Henry VIII, a large proportion seem to be clergy, monks and nuns.

Neil Bonser, Preston, Lancs

If there is an automatic exorcism process, it cannot be operating at Claydon church in Buckinghamshire, which is said to be haunted by the ghost of Sir Edmund Verney, the King's standard-bearer in the Civil War. He was last seen alive heroically fighting off a great mass of parliamentary troops at the Battle of Edgehill in 1643, and afterwards, all that could be found of his body among the slain was a single gloved hand still loyally clutching the royal standard.

King Charles I ordered that the severed part be taken back to Verney's home village at Claydon for burial in the parish church, and now, every year on the night of the anniversary of the battle, the ghostly figure of a soldier lacking one hand and dressed in seventeenth-century garb may be seen moving towards the place where Verney's hand is interred.

Michael Ghirelli, Buckingham, Bucks

What, if any, is the connection between Herne Bay in Kent, Herne Hill in south London and the pagan god Herne the Hunter?

While it is not impossible to identify some of the Celtic and Anglo-Saxon gods hidden in our place names, they do not show themselves so clearly as this name suggests. Earlier spellings often offer rather less romantic associations. The consensus is that the Old English word *hyrne*, meaning corner or angle, is the likely derivation. The term refers to a landscape feature. Herne Hill is in the corner or angle between the two hills either side. Herne Bay is in a corner of land by the sea and, in the eleventh century, there was a monastery 'aet hyrnan'.

Terry Lilly, Manchester Metropolitan University, Crewe

Terry Lilly asserts that the Herne in Herne Hill is 'in the corner or angle between two hills either side'. It wasn't so situated when I lived there for more than forty years.

Locals thought that Herne referred to Herons: just as the *OED* defines a hernet as a young heron.

Norman Shepherd, Bristol

I am happy to trade topographical memories of Herne Hill. When I lived in this part of south London forty years ago I would walk down Croxted Road to catch a bus up the hill called Herne, passing by the hill that dominates Brockwell Park and rises to over 125 ft, the two separated by the angle created by the now conduited River Effra.

I have no doubt that herons once fished that stream and I acknowledge the popular view of their recognition in the name. However, names are seldom what they appear to be from modern spelling. Even Heronbridge in Cheshire meant bridge at the river bend.

Sadly, much as we may wish it, neither Heron (from the Old French '*hairon*') nor *Hyrne* are signposts for our pagan god. I am perfectly content to think that Herne hunted the heron at the bend in the river Effra between the two hills – more romantic than the traffic maelstrom that flows there today.

Terry Lilly, Crewe, Cheshire

Terry Lilly's answer is feasible, however, Herne Bay hardly existed as a settlement before the nineteenth century and takes its name from the village of Herne, about two miles inland. Herne is considerably older. Its church dates from the fourteenth century. Some accounts state that the village name was originally spelt Heron and alludes to the fact that a heron was the crest of the local family of notables; but since the land rises steeply to the east and south of Herne village, and is level to the north and west, a derivation from the Old English *hyrne*, meaning corner, is more likely.

Wim Harthoorn, Horsham, West Sussex

There is no link. The place name is derived from an Anglo-Saxon word for a nook or a corner. Herne the Hunter, according to *Brewer's Dictionary of Phrase & Fable* (under the reference of 'Wild Huntsman') gives no origin for the name but reminds us it refers to the legendary keeper in Windsor forest.

In Shakespeare's *Merry Wives of Windsor*, Mistress Page sets up Falstaff to be dressed as Herne the Hunter, 'with a buck's head on him', and describes Herne's pranks: walking about, blasting trees, taking cattle, shaking chains 'in a hideous and dreadful manner'. Herne's Oak in Windsor Park was said to have been about 650 years old when it was blown down – and then replaced by Queen Victoria.

Len Snow, Wembley, Middx

The Australian film *Picnic at Hanging Rock* depicted

**the mysterious disappearance of a number of
schoolgirls on an outing, apparently round the
turn of the nineteenth century. Is there any
historical basis for the story?**

Apparently not. Although the author of the story, Joan
Lindsay, tantalizingly refused to reveal whether the events
were factual, there has never been any solid evidence in
the form of newspaper reports or historical records showing that the disappearances ever took place. They were
supposed to have taken place during a St Valentine's Day
picnic on Saturday 14 February 1900.

However, a check on the calendar shows that this date
was actually a Wednesday.

Lindsay does not explain what happened to the three
girls and their teacher who vanish while exploring the
rock during a college picnic, but there is an intriguing
suggestion that the book's imagery subtly indicates that
a sudden landslide buried them, leaving only a single
survivor.

David Morrow, London SW2

David Morrow says that '[Joan] Lindsay does not reveal
what happened to the three girls and their teacher'. In fact
the novel had a final chapter that the publishers excised,
feeling that the book was better without it. Released in
1987 after Lindsay's death, *The Secret of Hanging Rock*

gives the geologically lame explanation that they fell down a pothole whose entrance filled in afterwards, leaving no trace.

Ray Girvan, Topsham, Devon

In 1980, when I was press officer at Penguin Books, I wrote to (Lady) Joan Lindsay, author of *Picnic at Hanging Rock*, on behalf of a reader who had asked the same question. Her somewhat enigmatic reply stated:

> I have never actually kept count of the questions like this, in various languages, from all over the world! However I'm sure they have run into thousands! [It is] wonderful that readers of *Picnic* want this impossible question answered. It began shortly after *Picnic* was first published, and accelerated with the film, directed so beautifully by Peter Weir, with whom I never remember discussing the 'fact or fiction' question!

Jenny Wilford, Windsor, Berks

What are the rules of the game 'Mornington Crescent'?

I have no proof, but I believe that 'Mornington Crescent' is derived from the game 'Finchley Central', which was invented by John Conway (now Professor of Mathematics at Princeton University, but then a lecturer in Cambridge) around twenty years ago. 'Finchley Central' was invented as an example of a game with extremely simple rules that defies conventional game-theoretic analysis, and its rules are as follows: two players alternately name stations on the London Underground, and the first one to say 'Finchley Central' is the winner. However, in order to achieve a perfect win (which is worth infinitely more than an ordinary win), you must say 'Finchley Central' immediately before your opponent was going to say it. It seems quite probable that this game evolved into 'Mornington Crescent' as played on *I'm Sorry, I Haven't a Clue* but I have no information about the route by which it got there.

(Dr) P. T. Johnstone, Department of Pure Mathematics
and Mathematical Statistics, Cambridge

The origins of 'Mornington Crescent' have been most reliably traced to the old Gerry's Club in London's West End (now under new management). Among the regulars to whom Gerry's in the sixties was not so much a haunt as a home, the writer John Junkin has claimed authorship of the game. Nowadays, however, even Junkin is slow to divulge the rules, and the determined enquirer must have time and money on his side (about £20 ought to do it). For those who will stop at nothing, N. Stovold's *Rules And Origins* may be begged or stolen; but it has been out of print for years, and the British Library has drawn a blank on it. More fruitfully, though, the regulars of *I'm Sorry I Haven't a Clue* on Radio 4 can still be heard playing the original game to a high standard of elegance and cunning. Indeed, William Rushton's lethal mastery of Junkin's Parallel remains a joy to behold. I fear, though, that this is as much as can be said in print. The truth is that 'Mornington Crescent', like poker, can be played but seldom explained; its rules can be learnt but never taught; and its beauty should be noted but never queried.

Jon Magnusson, Producer,
BBC Radio Light Entertainment, London W1

When playing the underground version of 'Mornington Crescent', it is vital to remember that it was quite difficult to alight at 'Mornington Crescent' as most trains did not stop there.

C. S. Mence, New Malden, Surrey.

This question is really too tiresome to bother with a full answer, and in any case Samantha (the scorer) is probably the only person fully qualified to answer it in full. The questioner must just listen more carefully and work out the rules for himself.

Justin Downing, Sheffield

What do the pyramid and the eye represent on the American $1 note?

The device on the note is the reverse side of the Great Seal of the United States. The seal was adopted by Congress on 20 June 1782. Only the obverse was ever cut and put to use, although the design of the reverse still exists in theory. The symbols on both sides emerged after a long period of discussion, as analyzed very ably in *The Eagle and the Shield* by Richard Patterson and Richardson Dougall (Department of State, Washington, 1976). The symbols on the reverse are an unfinished pyramid of thirteen courses, an eye representing Providence, the date 1776 in Roman numerals and the mottoes: 'Annuit Coeptis' and 'Novus Ordo Seclorum'. The first is a phrase from Virgil and can be said to mean 'He favours our undertakings' – the 'he' being the deity represented by the eye. The second means 'A new order of the ages' and is also from Virgil. There is no doubt that the eye and the pyramid are Masonic in origin, and it seems likely that Francis Hopkinson, a Mason, was responsible for bringing these elements into the national emblems. The reverse of the seal was incorporated into the dollar bill by an act of President Roosevelt, dated 2 July 1935.

William G. Crampton, director,
The Flag Institute, Chester

The eye (or deity), in looking down on the pyramid, can see all of its sides equally (excluding the base) and as such is a representation of democracy. At any other corner, the eye could only see two of its faces.

David Shakespeare, London SW8

In Kurt Vonnegut's book, *Breakfast of Champions*, the author writes:

> If they [the Americans] studied their paper money for clues as to what their country was all about, they found, among a lot of other Baroque trash, a picture of a truncated pyramid with a radiant eye on top of it. Not even the President of the United States knew what it was all about. It was as though the country were trying to say to its citizens, 'IN NONSENSE IS STRENGTH'.

Daniel Jones, Northants

Robert Anton Wilson and Robert Shea, in their paranoid conspiracy novel, *Illuminatus*, quote the story that the Great Seal was given to Benjamin Franklin by a masked stranger who appeared in Franklin's garden one evening. American friends tell me this story is well known. (In fact, when I was at college, a fellow student checked every single reference from *Illuminatus* in the university library, and found them all to be genuine.) The masonic origin of the symbol is hardly surprising, given the connection between freemasonary and Liberal politics in the eighteenth century.

Daniel Jacobs, London NW4

Are the star dates in the Captain's Log in *Star Trek* in any chronological order?

In the original TV series the star dates were meant to be chronological, but delays in production of specific episodes, scheduling considerations, poor editing of scripts, etc., soon meant that star dates effectively became random numbers. There have been attempts to rationalize these dates along 'scientific' lines, where the date is explained to take account of faster-than-light travel and relativity. Some fans have adopted the international year–month–day–time format to try to explain the TV dates. However, none of these works for all the star dates in series. In the new TV series the star dates have the following format: 4Xyyy. yy where the '4' denotes the twenty-fourth century, 'X' the season (1 for the first, 2 for the second – currently showing – 3 for the third, etc.) and yyy. yy is a number between 000.00 and 999.99 to indicate the 'day'. However, this means that there are 1,000 'days' in a 'year' and only ten 'years' in a 'century'. Thus although a 'year' is more than three times longer than a solar year, a 'century' is less than a third the length of a solar century.

Chris Forman, Nottingham

Where do you draw the line?

Plimsoll got it right. If you ignore him, you're sunk.

David J. Nicolle, Bexley, Kent

You draw the line – or you used to draw the line – in the prize ring in the days of alfresco prize fighting. A line was scratched in the turf for each of the fighters to 'toe the line' at the beginning of each round. Fighters were not allowed to 'overstep the mark'. Fights were fought to a finish and, if a fighter was unable to toe the line because he did not feel 'up to scratch' he lost the contest.

Harry Humphreys, Lytham St Annes, Lancs

If the three wise men from the East followed a star to their east (Matthew, 2), how did they reach Bethlehem? They would have needed to follow a star to their west, surely.

Correct. The Magi did follow a star in a westerly direction, but let us not forget that they were, after all, wise men, and therefore probably not given to hasty actions. The Greek word *anatole* used by Matthew implies 'the direction of rising', so in rendering this as 'east' it should be understood as a general direction rather than a precise heading. It is not too fanciful to infer that they made further observations and deliberations over a lengthy period before concluding that the star (or whatever) was so portentous as to warrant following. By this time the object could well have been setting in the west, the direction in which the Magi eventually travelled.

Alan Linfield, Tring, Herts

It is a basic misunderstanding of navigation to imagine that one actually 'follows' a star. Imagine you are walking on the moors and can see a single tree some miles off. By walking towards it, you will remain on a constant compass bearing and eventually reach it. On the other hand, if you knew you wanted to head east, you could navigate by walking away from the tree, keeping it on a constant bearing on your compass. With the tree (or indeed a star) you follow a bearing rather than the object. Anyone can use a star to steer by. If you know you want to go north, just keep the Pole Star (Polaris, which happens to be almost exactly above the North Pole) ahead of you. If you want to go south, keep it on your back; east and you must keep it on your left shoulder. This is not very accurate, but for short distances, it might be good enough. Proper celestial navigation is more complicated, because all heavenly objects are in motion relative to an earthbound observer. The stars will appear to whirl round the sky because Earth spins daily on its axis. They change their apparent position with the seasons, as Earth tilts on its axis. They will seem to alter position according to the observer's latitude. The calculations required to compensate for their motions are very tricky. You will need a very accurate watch, a sextant, an almanac, a magnetic compass, a view of the horizon at sea level and knowledge of the equations to work it all out. The Three Wise Men had none of these.

Marcus Palliser, London W14

Seventh heaven. What are the other six?

In the cabbala, a Jewish mystical system of technology and metaphysics developed, mainly between the ninth and thirteenth centuries. It was maintained that there are seven heavens, each rising in happiness above the other. In this cosmology the lower heaven was the region of the stars; the highest, also known as the heaven of heavens, was the abode of God and the most exalted angels.

This classification passed into Islamic theology, in which the first heaven is of silver and in it are the stars, each with an angel warder and strung out like lamps on golden chains. This is the abode of Adam and Eve. The second heaven is of gold and the domain of Jesus and John the Baptist. The third is of pearl and allotted to Joseph; here Azrael writes the names of newborns in a large book from which he expunges the names of the newly dead.

The fourth heaven, of white gold, is Enoch's. Here dwells the Angel of Tears, who ceaselessly sheds tears for the sins of man. The fifth heaven is Aaron's and is of silver. The sixth heaven, which is of ruby and garnet, is presided over by Moses; here dwells the Guardian Angel of heaven and earth, half-snow and half-fire.

Geoffrey Taunton, Portsmouth

Geoffrey Taunton's answer was informative, but the cabbalistic version of the cosmos he describes was itself coopted from an ancient Greek concept. Their six concentrically nested heavenly spheres were supposed to be composed of an essential, crystalline substance, and to each was fixed one of the known heavenly bodies: Sun, Mercury, Venus, Mars, Jupiter and Saturn. The Moon occurred in the corrupted earthly realm, as evidenced by its visible blotches (the maria), and so was not accorded its own sphere. Seventh heaven, which became associated with the Judaeo-Christian Empyrean, occurred above the ultimate sphere encompassing and directing all the rest – the Primum Mobile.

Jim Costa, Museum of Comparative Zoology,
Cambridge, Mass, US

What is the evidence for St Brendan the navigator having 'sailed the Atlantic and discovered the New World' in the sixth century, as reportedly believed by a medieval linguist at the British Academy?

Brendan founded the monastery at Clonfert in AD 559 and died in AD 583. The earliest clear reference to his seafaring exploits is in Adamnan's life of St Columba – written around AD 670 – which mentions voyages to the Hebrides, Scotland and probably Brittany. The suggestion that he may have discovered the New World rests on the ninth-century *Voyage of St Brendan*, a book that circulated very widely in medieval Europe, influencing Columbus amongst others. The book tells how Brendan and thirty-three monks sailed over the seas to the Isle of the Blessed. Most of the detail is clearly drawn from the stock of sailors' yarns – from ancient Irish tales to Sinbad the Sailor – and it is doubtful whether any evidential value can be attached to it.

Tom Hennell, Withington, Cheshire

In 1976 Tim Severin and a crew of four sailed across the north Atlantic in a replica of St Brendan's ox-hide covered, wooden-framed, 36-ft vessel. The route was via Scotland, the Faroes and Iceland, and landfall was made in Newfoundland. Many of the key elements of the Brendan legend in the medieval text tallied with the places and creatures seen during the voyage. This is not, of course, proof that St Brendan discovered America but it does show such a voyage was possible and deserves to be given the same significance as Heyerdahl's Kon-Tiki voyage in its context. (Source: *The Brendan Voyage* by T. Severin, McGraw-Hill, 1978.)

Peter Sharp, Snells Beach, New Zealand

Where can I find peace of mind?

Alone, in the Grand Canyon at sundown.

Lissu Niemi, London NW4

Classical mysticism in general, eastern philosophy in particular, and yoga philosophy even more specifically, have suggested that peace of mind can be found in experiencing the fact that the real you (the true 'I') is in the mind. The mind, which by its nature is not capable of peace, is seen as a bundle of thoughts that usurps its position (as problem solver) and assumes the position of 'I' in the body. Many ancient myths symbolize this process with an unworthy imposter ousting the true ruler. The mythic story then involves the true ruler regaining the throne, with harmony being restored in the kingdom. Finding peace, which is a natural characteristic of the true 'I', is a matter of exposing the mind for what it is. Many methods are employed to do this, such as various meditation techniques; koans in Zen; dancing in sufism; chanting mantras; and self-surrender in devotional religion. Eternal peace of mind can only be found by understanding and experiencing the fact that you, in your essential nature, are not the mind.

Michael Dillon, Sheerness, Kent

Philippians, 4.4–7:

Rejoice in the Lord always. I will say it again: Rejoice! Let your gentleness be evident to all. The Lord is near. Do not be anxious about anything, but in everything, by prayer and petition, with thanksgiving, present your requests to God. And the peace of God, which transcends all understanding, will guard your hearts and your minds in Christ Jesus.

Stuart Stoner, Shoeburyness, Essex

Try the M4 West with London disappearing in the rearview mirror. It always works for me.

Jeff Williams, Ystrad Mynach, Mid-Glamorgan

On the eastbound carriageway three miles west of M4 junction 13 is a large exit labelled 'Works Access Only'. It leads to a road, not marked on any map,

that disappears over a hill. The millennium map on the internet shows a large array of rectangular structures. Is it anything I should worry about?

Locals maintain that this slip road leads to RAF Welford, which was used as a base by the US during the cold war. This would explain the rectangular shapes on the millenium map – they are missile silos.

My mother, who lives near Newbury, has always maintained that the cruise missiles, allegedly at nearby Greenham Common, were in fact based at Welford. This would make sense, if only in terms of transport logistics. Cruise missiles were designed to be mobile and capable of being launched from any part of the country. To reach the M4 from Greenham (in the eighties) necessitated driving through Newbury, whereas Welford has its own private slip road.

Perhaps all the women who so persistantly protested against the cruise missiles were actually camping in the wrong place after all.

Jackie Nickson, Farncombe, Surrey

Many 'Access Only' roads are in fact motorway police stations and garages. A couple of years ago, I was given a lift to Luton airport by a Met police detective. He swung off the motorway on to one of these roads, promising that it would take many miles off the journey – which it did.

Some way up this road, there were rectangular structures, an array of parked police vehicles and officers relaxing with tea and fags. Anyone wishing to try these shortcuts, however, should be advised that you need someone in the car who can show a warrant card.

Graham White, Milton Bridge, Midlothian

RAF Welford and its private slip-road off the M4 were no secret to peace campaigners of the eighties, as Jackie Nickson implies. It was well known as Europe's largest munitions store, although the military were not unnaturally reticent to discuss exactly what was kept there. There were a number of temporary peace camps outside its gates and at least one letter was delivered to the single British officer on the site.

Unlike Greenham, there is very little space for a camp outside Welford, whose publicly accessible gate is on an unclassified road with little or no passing traffic. However, the US personnel were clearly alarmed at finding themselves targeted and I witnessed one unsuccessful attempt by a driver to mount the verge and flatten a campaigner's tent.

Dave Headey, Faringdon, Oxon

Munitions used to be moved in and out of this US army depot annually, so that their use-by date did not expire. In the 1970s I worked for a large firm of hauliers involved in transporting munitions, which, my drivers told me, were mainly bombs that did not have fuses and were consequently harmless. All the drivers were given rudimentary safety instructions and a fire extinguisher, but when one of my drivers asked what to do in the case of a fire, he was told to run. We used to take the munitions to other US bases in the UK and also to south Wales to be put on ships to return the munitions to America.

Peter Jenkins, Dorking, Surrey

The routing of the M4 was decided largely by the US government as part of the missile distribution system. The instigation of the Newbury bypass and other work on the A34 was for the same purpose. It is ironic that the work was done so long after its real purpose had ceased to exist in order to save face and conceal military involvement. Perhaps the US Freedom of Information Act will reveal something soon. Our own papers will presumably be secret for at least thirty years.

John Batts, Banbury, Oxon

Let me assure your readers that the Greenham Women were not 'camping in the wrong place'. RAF Greenham Common Airbase, occupied by the United States Airforce, began receiving ninety-six ground launch cruise missiles in November 1983. They were taken to Salisbury Plain at least once a month to prepare for nuclear war: each time they left we tracked them down and interrupted and disrupted the exercise. We saw these weapons flown out in 1992.

RAF Welford was also occupied by USAF but was a depository for so-called 'conventional' bombs. This was verified by Greenham Women when they took action against RAF Welford on a number of occasions, especially in 1986 when the USAF, stationed at Upper Heyford, bombed Libya with cluster bombs from Welford. Women painted these bombs with red paint, as a symbolic act, to denote the spilling of blood. The security within Welford was not the same as is found in a nuclear establishment.

Sarah Hipperson, Greenham Common
Women's Peace Camp, London E11

John Batts need not resort to the US Freedom of Information Act to ascertain who influenced the route of the M4 in Berkshire – the statutory processes were completed in 1968, so the papers have been outside the thirty-year limit for some time. But he will search in vain for evidence to support his allegation of US government involvement. I was a Ministry of Transport civil servant heavily involved in advising ministers on the route. The heaviest lobbying came from the racehorse trainers and members of the House of Lords – who seemed to form the majority of the population of the 'Royal' County of Berkshire – but there was not a word from Dr Strangelove.

The Welford depot was served by the truncated remains of the Lambourn railway branch line. This closed to passengers in 1960 but the Newbury–Welford section remained open specifically to serve the base, and this continued after the adjacent section of the M4 was opened in 1971. I understand the decline of British rail freight in the mid-seventies led to the US forces' wish to shift the traffic to road, leading to the building of the slip-road and closure of the railway. This may be the source of Mr Batts' unfounded suspicion.

Reginald Dawson, Tywyn, Gwynedd

About twenty years ago, at an annual meeting with a visiting government minister, I raised the great concern of residents in villages such as Great Shefford about the large munition lorries that thundered through their roads at all hours of the day and night to and from the US Airforce base at Welford, just north of the M4. Minister Lynda Chalker asked what, if anything, could be done, and agreed to consider my suggestion of private access roads between the base and the M4. I was most impressed when she replied two weeks later that after studying the proposal in detail, she was proceeding with it! The villagers were delighted at the outcome of cooperative politics. So was I!

Trevor Brown (retired county councillor), Newbury, Berks

Is it true that Berwick-upon-Tweed is still at war with the Russians?

Because of its status as a disputed border city between England and Scotland, Berwick was listed a separate entity on declarations of war and peace treaties. At the outbreak of the Crimean war, Berwick duly appeared as one of the belligerents taking on the Russian Empire, but in the Treaty Of Paris, 1856, ending the war, Berwick was left out, hence the continuing state of hostilities.

In 1968, however, Berwick decided to end this crippling conflict and signed a peace treaty with the Soviet Union (who gamely went along with exercise). At the accompanying civic event, the Mayor of Berwick is reputed to have assured the Soviet ambassador that 'from now on, the Russians can sleep safely in their beds'.

Tom Seldon, Liverpool

In *Journey To The Centre Of The Earth*, Jules Verne mentions 'the theory of an English captain' that the Earth is a hollow sphere containing an atmosphere made luminous by pressure in which two stars orbit. Further details anyone?

Verne's reference is to Captain John Cleves Symmes, who thought he had scientifically shown that the Earth is hollow. He argued the case on grounds of 'cosmic parsi-mony': a hollow Earth represents 'a great saving of stuff' compared with a solid Earth. An expedition was sent to the South Pole to find the hole that Symmes claimed was there, but it had to turn back before getting south of Chile. Symmes died in 1829. (Source: Robert Anton Wilson's *Cosmic Trigger, Volume 2*.)

Kevin Keenoy, London

In his book *The New Apocrypha*, John Sladek describes two kinds of Hollow Earth theory. The most popular is the one used by Jules Verne. The second theory was put forward by a nineteenth-century American, Cyrus 'Koresh' Tedd, who claimed we live inside a bubble of rock. He said that the Sun revolved to show its light and dark sides. The Sun rising and setting and the presence of the Moon, stars and planets in the night sky were explained by a set of optical laws that also explained why we can't see over the horizon.

Michael Dunn, South Shields, Tyne and Wear

I have heard of a hill, somewhere in the UK, that one's car will actually roll up. Does this exist? If so, is it an optical illusion, a magnetic phenome-non, or what?

Yes there is: on the A719, between Dunure and Croy Bay is the 'Electric Brae', known locally as Croy Brae. Rising 17 ft west to east there is a slope of 1 in 86 upwards from the bend at the Glen. The configuration of the land on either side of the road provides an optical illusion, making it look as if the slope is going the other way. Therefore, a stationary car on the road, with the brakes off, will appear to move slowly uphill. The term 'Electric Brae' dates from a time when it was incorrectly thought to be a phenomenon caused by electric or magnetic attraction within the Brae. Go there if you can – it is truly wonderful. Take some golf balls with you and drop them out of your window to see which way they roll.

Matthew Payne, Hampton

It is an optical illusion and is actually not uncommon. I have never been at the UK one but have been to Magnetic Hill in New Brunswick, Canada, and to a similar phenomenon outside Shenyang in north-east China.

David Crawford, Toronto, Canada

On the A53 halfway between Newcastle-under-Lyme and Shrewsbury is the village of Loggerheads. Nearby, on my map, there is a battle site dated 1459. Is this at all related to the phrase 'to be at loggerheads'?

The *Concise Oxford Dictionary* gives the meaning of 'log-ger' in this connection as 'a block of wood for hobbling a horse'. Thus a horse that was hobbled would not be able to move and hence two people in a dispute, who will not budge, would effectively be hobbled or at loggerheads.

There is another place named Loggerheads, near Mold, in Clwyd, on the River Alun. In a pub there, the Logger-heads Inn, is a plaque describing a dispute between two farmers that claims to give the place its name. I would sus-pect that some local dispute, or battle, also gave its name to the Staffordshire village.

Rosemary Bentley, Egham, Surrey

Loggerheads were the heraldic symbols by which the ownership of military battering rams was established during the middle ages. Since the battering rams used by armies in the pay of the English crown carried the head of a leopard, in the medieval royal arms, the full open-mouthed cat's face of a heraldic leopard came to be called a loggerhead.

Quite how three leopard loggerheads came to be incor-porated in the heraldic device appropriated to Shropshire is a bit obscure. They do not seem to have come from the arms of the various earls of Shrewsbury. The eleventh- and twelfth-century earls are unlikely to have borne armo-rial devices. John Talbot, created earl in 1442, had two lions rampant in two quarters of his shield, two lions passant in a third and some birds, probably from the Valence arms, in the fourth. They are much more likely to have derived from some grant after one of the many sieges the town of Shrewsbury endured during the Welsh wars.

What is certain is that the name of the village of Loggerheads, the arms of the county, and the phrase 'to be at loggerheads' are related. They are all to do with battering rams.

The battle of Blore Heath, east of Market Drayton, was fought on 14 September 1459. A Lancastrian army commanded by James Touchet, Lord of Audley near Stoke and of Cemais in West Wales was pursuing a Yorkist force less than half its size, commanded by Richard Neville, Earl of Salisbury. Fighting from behind palisades erected overnight at the top of a slope above the muddy bed of the Hempnill Brook and with two well-placed bands of archers, the Yorkists demolished the Lancastrian attack.

Touchet was killed by Roger Kynaston of Hordley while attempting to turn the Yorkist position from the north. Battering rams, a weapon of siege operations, could have been no possible use in the battle.

Michael Eastham, Fishguard, Pembrokeshire

By the side of the track at Colwich, Staffs, on the west coast main line, is an ancient sign with an

arrow pointing north carrying the words 'To Crewe and the North'. For whose benefit is this sign?

The sign concerned is at Colwich junction on the west coast main line, between Lichfield and Stafford. This is the junction where the direct line to Manchester via Stoke on Trent and Macclesfield, operated by the old North Staffordshire Railway, diverges from the old London and North Western Railway main line to Crewe and Carlisle.

The sign is for the information of travellers on the diverging line to Stoke who might want to know where the important-looking line they were leaving in fact led to. I believe there was a corresponding sign on the opposite side of the former North Staffordshire line indicating 'To Stoke on Trent and Manchester' for the information of Crewe-bound passengers.

There is (or was) a similar sign at Euxton Junction, south of Preston. Here the former Lancashire and Yorkshire line branched off from the main line, heading towards Chorley, Bolton and Manchester. The sign by the diverging tracks read: 'To Bolton and Manchester'.

Signs for the information of passengers exist at major railway summits, e.g. Shap or Beattock, giving the height above sea level, but the passenger has to be alert to see them as these are passed at high speed. Other examples are border signs, such as the one just north of Berwick on the east coast main line, which says 'Welcome to Scotland' on one side, and 'Haste Ye Back' on the other.

Philip Heyes, Wigan, Lancs

It's to direct the wretched passengers who have to walk it when the train breaks down.

Brian Saperia, Harrow, Middx

Travelling from Ulverston station in Cumbria could be a hazardous matter. On the platform there used to be an unnerving large iron sign, with an arrow pointing south to PRESTON AND BEYOND.

Adrian Cunningham, Lancaster

What did William Blake have in mind when he used the expression 'dark satanic mills'?

The phrase was used in the preface to *Milton* (1804) and refers not to the new cotton mills or factories but, as David Erdman suggests (*Blake: Prophet Against Empire* [3rd edn, 1977], p 396), to the 'mills that produce dark metal, iron and steel, for diabolic purposes'. At the time London was 'a major war arsenal and the hub of the machinery of war' – the war against the French had been renewed in 1803 after a brief peace – and Blake's symbolism was part of what Erdman calls Blake's 'determination to forge counterarms of art' (p 395).

Keith McClelland, London N4

Who lives at No. 9 Downing Street?

Nobody lives at No. 9, but there is a door that goes into the Privy Council building from Downing Street. It is not well marked and is secluded from the view of anybody standing at the palatial gates at the bottom of Downing Street.

Lawrence Brennan, Ampleforth College, York

If I were to travel a complete circuit of the M25, how many miles would I save by driving anti-clockwise as opposed to clockwise?

The distance saved is not dependent on the length of the circuit but only on the width of the separation between the two carriageways. In fact it is 2[pi] times the average separation. The answer depends on which lane the driver uses. In the inside lane, supposing each lane is 3 metres wide and the central reservation is 6 metres across the distance saving is 2[pi] × ((5 × 3) + 6) = 142 metres. Observation shows, though, that in practice no one uses the inside lane on the M25. More probably, the journeys will be made in the two 'fast' lanes, which are separated by just 9 metres. This means a saving of 2[pi] × 9, or only 57 metres out of a circuit length of roughly 200 kilometres.

Peter Telford, Redhill, Surrey

Peter Telford is much mistaken. His formula would only apply if the route round the M25 formed a perfect circle, which it does not. Part of this motorway may be in circular form but there will be straight sections. Assuming that these were to turn off at right angles, the distance saved would be eight times the separation, as opposed to 6.28 times the separation for the circle. So the factors will change constantly, depending on the radius of the road at any given point. Theoretically, it is almost impossible to calculate the exact mileage saved, and the only practical way is to drive round both routes and take the difference in distances. However, I can assure you that the distance saved would be a very small fraction of the actual distance travelled.

Christiaan Jonkers, Stourbridge, West Mids

I must defend Peter Telford and challenge Christiaan Jonkers. The distance saved is indeed twice [pi] times the average separation, and can be proved mathematically to be so. Further, the circuit does not have to be a circle, or anything like one. All that is needed is that the curve followed by the motorway be sufficiently smooth (that is, that the curves have large radius compared to the turning circle of the car), and motorways with sharp corners are not too popular with the Department of Transport. Whether or not there are straight sections is a complete red herring. Actually, there is just one thing that might disturb the calculations. They do assume that the motorway is flat (planar). But I doubt that the ups and downs affect the final answer all that much, since again they are never too drastic.

(Dr) Peter McMullen, Department of Mathematics,
University College London

Much as I dislike disagreeing with a colleague, I feel that I must do so. Dr McMullen ignores an important factor. A simple consequence of Pythagoras's Theorem is that over-taking manoeuvres usually result in drivers travelling further. Due to this, there can be considerable variability in the total distance travelled between successive circuits of a ring road, even for journeys made in the same direction. Although pure mathematics could be used to estimate the effects this would have on journeys around the M25, perhaps someone should experiment.

(Dr) Stephen Gallivan, Department of Statistical Research,
University College London

If we allow the Earth to be a perfect sphere, then the

quantity twice [pi] times the carriageway separation is too much. A correction equal to four times [pi] times the area of London (i.e. enclosed by the M25) divided by the area of the Earth must be subtracted.

Jonathan Fine, Huntingdon, Cambs

You cannot travel a complete circuit of the M25. The motorway gives way to the A282 at the approaches to the Dartford Tunnel.

T. J. Allen, Hindhead, Surrey

A friend and I decided to experiment. We first calibrated our milometers to make certain they read the same distance for a stretch of road, and then I drove clockwise and my friend anticlockwise on the M25. Our starting and finishing point was the South Mimms service station. The result was surprising: clockwise 120.30 miles, anticlockwise 120.80 miles. We agreed that we would stay in the slow lane as far as possible, only moving to the middle lane when appropriate. Neither of us used the outer, fast lane. However, the discrepancy of 0.5 miles seems to have occurred because of a diversion on the anticlockwise circuit, immediately south of the Dartford Tunnel. So, at the moment, it is a shorter journey to take the clockwise carriageway, especially if travelling to Kent or Essex.

Penelope Edwards, London N2

I fear that Penelope Edwards and her friend have wasted both time and money in driving round the M25. A car's odometer only measures to the nearest 0.1 mile and, even if you can estimate distances by the partial change of the numbers, it cannot be better than 0.05 miles. Calibrating the odometers of the two cars against one another will not help because of this basic inaccuracy in the odometer's mechanism. If the distance over which they drove to calibrate them was 10 miles, then their calibration will be accurate to 0.05 miles in 10 miles, equivalent to 0.6 miles over the complete 120-mile trip; greater than the difference they found. Even if they had used the same car for the two trips, removing the need for calibration, it is unlikely that the result would be any more reliable, since the same trip made in the same car will not necessarily give the same measured distance every time. The basic problem is one that affects every scientist or engineer carrying out a measurement: the equipment must be able to measure smaller than the quantity being measured. Otherwise, it's like using a tape measure to find the diameter of a human hair.

Dudley Turner, Westerham, Kent

Who actually owns Buckingham Palace? It was purchased by King George III in 1761 and passed to his son, George IV. But I have been told that

the wills of George III and George IV have never been settled.

Under the Land Registration Act 1988, anyone is entitled to find out the ownership of registered land in England and Wales. Of some twenty-two million properties and plots of land in England and Wales, more than thirteen million are registered – although the remaining nine million are not. Assuming that Buckingham Palace is registered, then you can find out the identity of the freeholder for a fee of £12. A leaflet on the procedure is available from HM Land Registry.

David Northmore (author, The Freedom Of Information Handbook*), London*

I doubt very much that the Land Register will answer the question. While land in central London has been subject to registration since the end of the nineteenth century, registration is only effective if there is a 'dealing' with the land within the meaning of the various land registration acts. By and large, this means that there has to have been a sale of the land, for a transmission on death effective by an 'assent' does not need to be registered. I suspect that the title to Buckingham Palace is not registered, for it has apparently been in the ownership of the same family for nearly 230 years. This is always assuming that the family has not sold the palace, say, to the Property Services

Agency or one of its predecessors in recent years. For this reason, the register is unlikely to reveal the ownership of property belonging to old landed families generally.

Thomas C. Sutton & Co, Solicitors,
Bishop Auckland, Co Durham

Who were the Seven Sisters, and why did they have a road in North London named after them?

The sisters were elm trees surrounding a single walnut tree by High Road, Tottenham. The walnut tree is first recorded by the Vicar of Tottenham from 1607–32. He noted that it flourished without growing bigger and was popularly associated with the burning of an unknown Protestant. However, he did not refer to the Seven Sisters by their name, which is not recorded until a licence was sought for lopping their lower branches in 1732. The walnut died by 1790. When a new road was built from Holloway north-eastwards across open country, to link the West End of London with Tottenham in 1833, it was named after its destination, for the trees were sited close by the junction of Seven Sisters Road and Tottenham High Road, but they have long since disappeared. All this information has been obtained from the *Victoria County History of Middlesex, Volume V*.

Malcolm A. Stokes, London N6

During the Second World War, a German-language newspaper, *Die Zeitung*, was on sale in the Welsh village where I was evacuated. Why, and what happened to it?

Die Zietung was conceived in the summer of 1940, at the time of the Battle of Britain, and first published on 12 March 1941. From 2 January 1942, a twelve-page weekly replaced the original four-page daily newspaper. The last edition appeared on 1 June 1945.

Die Zeitung was created by and for German-speaking refugees, but boycotted by some socialists in exile until late in 1944. It saw itself as the only free, independent German-language newspaper in Europe and perceived Britain, in the light of Germany's invasion of its neighbouring territories, as the last free haven in Europe. The newspaper was given the approval of the British government.

In what it published in its political, economic and cultural sections, *Die Zeitung* opposed Hitler in every way it deemed possible. The editors were soon encouraged to distribute the newspaper abroad. The success of the subsequent 'overseas edition' is reflected in its own transformation from an eight-page fortnightly newspaper into a twelve-page weekly.

In June 1945, with Hitler's Germany defeated, *Die Zeitung* declared that it had reached its goal and ceased publication. The editors felt that the tasks facing journalists in postwar Germany should be tackled by a different newspaper. *Die Zeitung* had always been regarded as a wartime initiative.

A full set of the British *Zeitung* is available for consultation in the National Library of Scotland in Edinburgh.

Despite the paper shortages facing the country, the government of the day permitted several foreign-language newspapers to be printed in London – a situation eventually challenged in parliament in June 1943.

(Dr) Donal McLaughlin, Department of Languages,
Heriot-Watt University, Edinburgh

The title Duke of Clarence was used by British royals up to the unfortunate son of Queen Victoria. But where or what is the origin of the title? Clarence isn't in any atlas I can find.

The title derives from the little village of Clare in Suffolk, on the A1092 near Long Melford. William the Conqueror gave it to Richard FitzGilbert, whose descendants, the de Clare family, became Earls of Clare, Hertford and Gloucester. County Clare in Ireland is named after them. The tenth and last earl, Gilbert de Clare, was killed at the Battle of Bannockburn. His lands were inherited by his grandniece, Elizabeth de Burgh, who married Lionel of

Antwerp, second son of Edward III. He was granted the title Duke 'of Clarence', meaning 'of the lands of the de Clare family'. The estates reverted to the Crown when his descendant Edward IV became king, and 'Clarence' has been used as one of the titles for royal dukes ever since. Its holders either seem to become Kings, like George III's son, William IV, or die without founding a line, like Queen Victoria's unfortunate grandson, Prince Eddie.

C. V. Gidlow, Faversham, Kent

Contrary to C. V. Gidlow's reply, County Clare in Ireland is not, in fact, named after the de Clare family. The name comes from the town of Clare (now Clarecastle), in Irish *An Clar*, meaning 'the level place'.

Martyn Cornell, Isleworth, Middx

I saw a temporary road sign on the A28 in Kent that read: 'Statutory undertakers diversions taking place.' What did it mean?

It was a dead end.

Ron Taylor, London SW19

It may sound slightly bizarre, but the 'undertakers' in question are actually the public energy companies, like gas, electricity, water and also telephones, which undertake services for the public. They have a legal and thus a statutory right to dig up the road to mend their apparatus – causing much annoyance and nuisance to the rest of us.

Len Snow, Wembley, Middx

In the UK there are motorways M1–6, M8 and M9. But why no M7?

When main roads were first numbered it was decided to make the Great North Road (London–Edinburgh) the A1. Five other key roads from London were chosen to be A2–A6 and these were numbered consecutively, clockwise from the A1, making the road to Dover the A2, to Portsmouth the A3, and so on. A- and B-class roads were then numbered so that their first digit was taken from the segment in which they were situated, so that roads between the A1 and the North Sea coast were numbered beginning with '1' (i.e. London–Norwich became the A11). This was repeated in the other segments. A similar arrangement pertained in Scotland with roads from Edinburgh, the A7 being assigned to the road to Carlisle, the A8 to Glasgow and the A9 to the far north. Again roads were numbered according to the segment they were in, so that all the roads on the Western Isles have numbers beginning with '8'.

When it came to numbering the motorways, the decision was taken to make the first major motorway the M1. Other motorways were numbered because they ran parallel to the equivalent main road, i.e. the M2 and the M6 (at its north end at least), or headed off in the same general direction, such as the M3. The clear exception here is the M5, which goes nowhere near either London or Holyhead. In Scotland, the M8 and M9 parallel their respective A roads. As far as the '7' segment is concerned, of the three motorways in that segment, two (the M74 and the M77) parallel their equivalent A road while the M73 runs in the same direction as the A73. There are (as yet) no plans to build a motorway from Edinburgh to Carlisle, so we are unlikely to have an M7 for the foreseeable future.

Charles Tremeer, Bedlington, Northumberland

What happened to the *Mary Celeste* after she was found abandoned?

She was eventually taken back to New York and sold. The new owner sent her to Montevideo with a cargo of lumber. This appears to have been a pretty disastrous voyage: the ship lost some of her cargo and rigging in a storm on the way out and most of her living cargo of horses and mules (and the skipper!) on the return trip. Thereafter, she changed hands frequently, continuing to ply the American coastline and suffering a series of further mishaps. In 1884, she was acquired by one Gilman C. Parker, who, together with co-conspirators, decided to attempt finally to make some profit from the jinxed vessel. She was loaded with a cargo of junk registered as high-class merchandise and insured for $27,000, deliberately grounded on a coral reef in the Haitian Gulf of Gonave and set on fire, after the cargo and crew had been brought ashore. A claim was duly filed but the suspicious insurance companies sent investigators to question the crew. Parker and three of his partners were subsequently tried in Boston on a charge of barratry but freed because of a hung jury, though they never collected their insurance money. Eight months later, Parker died in disrepute and poverty; one of his associates was sent to a lunatic asylum and another committed suicide. The jinx pursued the *Mary Celeste* to the very end. For more details see John Godwin's book *This Baffling World* (Bantam, 1973).

Philip J. Evison, London SW15

ODD PLACES

Which single clock face tells the greatest number
of people the time on any given day?

That would be the one in the Piccadilly-circus of
Microsoft Windows. Sadly .

Stephen Fry, 'Paperback Original'

The Sun.

Has anybody actually driven their car .
because the sign at the entrance to a village said
them to?

As children on holiday in Caerphilly we had great fun
writing 'Please Drive . ' on all the signs at the entrance

Which single clock face tells the greatest number of people the time on any given day?

That would be the one in the bottom-right corner of Microsoft Windows. Sadly.

Stephen Rigby, Woodford Green, Essex

The Sun.

Tony Lunn, Uxbridge, Middx

Has anybody actually driven more carefully because the sign at the entrance to a village asks them to?

As children on holiday in Caerphilly we had great fun writing 'Please Drive . . .' on all the signs at the entrance to the town. I don't know if we contributed to a lowering of road accidents or not.

Jon Potter, London W4

Yes. And I've also been about to gratuitously ram the car in front when, just in time, I've spotted a 'Baby On Board' sign.

Paul Dennehy, Enfield, Middx

Paul Dennehey has mistaken the purpose of baby-on-board signs. They are not a vain plea for drivers to drive more carefully. They are a warning to emergency rescue crews that in a serious accident they should also be looking for a small being who might be wedged out of sight or flung some distance from the scene of the crash. Accidents in the 30mph zone of this small village are practically a daily event.

Paul Jackson, Etchingham, East Sussex

With reference to Paul Jackson's reply, does he seriously believe people with baby-on-board signs take them down when the baby is not in the car? How many hours are spent in fruitless search after accidents by people looking for apparently vaporized small beings?

Colin Hall, Broughty Ferry, Dundee

This query reminded me of the following musings by philosopher Ludwig Wittgenstein:

> Nothing seems to me less likely than that a scientist or mathematician who reads me should be seriously influenced in the way he works. In that respect my reflections are like the notices on the ticket offices at English railway stations [during the Second World War]: 'Is your journey really necessary?' As though someone who read this would think, 'On second thoughts, no'.

Helen Tookey, Liverpool

At the entrance to a small village near us in north Cornwall, the sign reads 'Slow Down for Fox Sake'. Hopefully, this causes you to slow down while you think about it, and when the penny drops, find it amusing enough to take note.

Sylvia Henry, north Cornwall

On leaving, we often read the sign thanking us for driving safely through the village. Should we then start driving dangerously and speeding?

Gordon Joly, London

As you enter the village of Silverstone, there is a large, clear sign: 'Silverstone welcomes careful drivers'. Nuff said?

Chris Coombs, Wakefield, Yorks

Why has Westward Ho! got an exclamation mark?

Westward, ho! was the trail bosses' shout as the wagon train set off from the eastern parts of the US to the west, where the pioneers would settle.

Amanda Clay, Norman, Oklahoma, US

The area is named after Charles Kingsley's book of the same name. The book is thought to be the first that uses an exclamation mark.

Toby Wilson, Teddington, Middx

Why is Britain a nation of tea-drinkers and America of coffee-drinkers?

I think this is to do with geography and immigration. America drank tea until independence (witness the Boston tea party) and European immigrants introduced a taste for coffee. England by contrast had long participated in the tea trade – a product of the British empire. Tea was simply more lucrative than coffee for sale in the UK and therefore the big tea merchants pushed sales of tea rather than coffee.

Colin Watson, Aberdeen

This business about the Boston tea party is an urban myth. Consider how much further a pound of tea goes, and how much more can be compressed into a given space, than coffee. Tea was widely drunk in the US away from the seaboards until the railroads made it economical to move coffee in large quantities. Before then coffee was just too expensive for most people. That it was once a luxury made it desirable to the masses once it became available. These same conditions pertain on the Pampas, where mate is still drunk for the same reasons as tea once was in the US.

Peter Brooke, Kinmuck, Scotland

Can you calculate a country's cultural worth? If so, which country in the world can be said to have the greatest cultural worth?

It depends a little on how you define culture. South America and the Middle East have the oldest civilizations and some of the most magnificent artefacts, but the works tend to be more functional than art for art's sake. Britain has a lot of well-preserved monumental history, spanning around 6,000 years. It also has much art for pleasure, from Beowulf onwards. If a purely verbal culture is sufficient, then the native North American tribes had stories and sagas that few Europeans could have competed with. Finally, the most 'mythic' culture in the world has to be

Greece. The sheer depth and range of their compositions is amazing.

John Smith, Stockport

I imagine it must be Italy. Taking into account painting, sculpture, literature and architecture from medieval times, the country should win hands down. And that's without adding their Roman heritage. But what about the UK? Why has our country excelled in so many areas, but not to the same extent as other countries in terms of culture? (Please don't use Shakespeare as an answer to all of our cultural deficiencies.)

David Colville, Glasgow

New College was founded in the thirteenth century. What is the oldest thing we call new?

The New Forest dates back to 1079. The Vikings visited Newfoundland as early as 1001, but it was not settled until the seventeenth century.

Hugh Venables, Southampton

Naples was founded by Greeks in the eighth century BC and was named Neapolis – new city.

Rob Horton, Birmingham

The neolithic (Greek for new stone-age) period started in south-west Asia in about 10,000 BC.

Matt Heath, Nottingham

A nova. It may be new to us, but some exploded tens of millions of years ago.

Christopher Woods, Mt Victoria, NSW, Australia

The neoproterozoic, or period of new primitive life, the last part of the pre-Cambrian, spans roughly 1,000 to 540 million years ago.

Jeremy Young, Tonbridge

Why do the British drive on the left and other countries on the right?

The left is the natural side to ride if you are on horseback. Mounting a horse is done from the left, so that a sword (worn on the left by right-handed men) will not get in the way. If you mount from a mounting block or the verge on the left, it is natural to set off on the left-hand side of the road.

Christine Moore, London SW4

There is a theory that the change to the right came about with firearms, which are fired from the right shoulder, thus aimed to the left. Certainly a major proponent of keeping to the right was Napoleon Bonaparte, who whether for military reasons or personal custom, imposed keeping to the right wherever he went. In the twentieth century it was another dictator that imposed keeping to the right wherever he went: Adolf Hitler. In his birthplace in Austria and in Czechoslovakia signs reading *Rechts fahren* (drive right) were put up when the Nazis moved in. So by keeping to the left we are sticking to our British independence.

Noel Ellis, London SE15

Implicit in the question is the suggestion that Britain is alone in this particular practice. In fact, over forty countries drive on the left.

Nicholas Pritchard, Southampton

Where, when and by whom were semi-detached houses first built?

I do not know where the first semi-detached house was built but I have it on reliable authority that the second one was built just next door to the first.

George James, Shepperton, Middx

The origin of the semi-detached house, at least in London, is explained in *The Book of London*, which I edited for Weidenfeld last year. The Georgian terrace held sway until the last decade of the eighteenth century, when inflationary pressures pushed up building costs and left some terraces uncompleted – similar to the problems to-day in Docklands. Building houses in self-contained pairs meant that it was easier to stop when the money ran out. The architect and developer, Michael Searles, is credited with London's earliest semis, built in Kennington Park Road in the early 1790s. He followed these with a development in Greenwich and the Paragon in Blackheath. Then, as now, south London was at the cutting edge of innovation.

Michael Leapman, London SW8

Michael Leapman is nearly there – but not quite. Architect Michael Searles (a Greenwich man) may well have been inspired by the pair of houses built in Blackheath in 1776 by Thoman Gayfere and John Groves, both of Westminster. The houses, which stand today on the west edge of the heath and are known as Lydia and Sherwell, are, by legend, the first semi-detached houses certainly in London. That is, if you take the meaning of semi-detached to be two houses consciously designed to look from a distance like one. Pevsner/Cherry in their book, *London 2: South*, give the Gayfere/Groves houses the accolade. It is a credit that we at the Blackheath Society will stoutly defend. Searles's first semis followed about thirty years later. But if it is the terrace form in question, then Searles is your man.

Neil Rhind for The Blackheath Society, London SE5

Sorry Blackheath! Richard Gillow of Lancaster (1734–1811) was designing 'semis' or pairs of houses in that town as early as 1758–9, in Moor Lane. The earliest identifiable surviving pair is that built in 1760 at Fleet Bridge (now facing the bus station and partly demolished) for Captain Henry Fell. These are very similar to a pair in St Leonardsgate which may be the buildings designed by Gillow in 1765–6 for Edward Salisbury. Captain Fell occupied one of his houses himself but the others were built to be let. Gillow obtained estimates of £110 for building William Braithwaite's houses in Moor Lane in 1759 and reckoned they would let for £4 per annum each.

Pace Pevsner, no legend here: the evidence is in the Gillow archives in Westminster Public Library. Richard Gillow was the son of the founder of the cabinet-making dynasty, and seems to have studied architecture in London. From 1757 to the 1770s, he provided designs for numerous public and private buildings in the Lancaster area. The architectural work of Richard Gillow was the subject of my dissertation in 1982. I used the Gillow archives to establish beyond doubt that Richard Gillow designed a considerable number of buildings in this period.

P. A. Harrison, London SW16

Sorry, Blackheath! Sorry, Richard Gillow of Lancaster. What must surely be counted as the first pair of semi-detached houses, nos 808–10 Tottenham High Road, London N17, date from 1715–25 – thus predating Gillow's work by something like fifty years. This pair of houses makes a noble and remarkably balanced visual ensemble still, despite later shopfronts. For an illustration, see Dan Cruickshank and Peter Wyld's fascinating *London: the Art of Georgian Building*.

Philip Maher, Marston, Oxford

It was always my belief that the semi-detached dwelling originated in the ancient Inca civilization of South America. This novel idea greatly impressed the Spanish Conquistadores, who brought the concept to Europe in the sixteenth century, and gave it the name 'Casa Doble'.

Vaughan R. Hully, Warley, West Mids.

Summerson's *Georgian London* states that the Eyre Estate in St John's Wood 'was the first part of London, and indeed of any other town, to abandon the terrace house for the semi-detached villa – a revolution of striking significance and far-reaching effect'. One reason why the semi-detached house was so frequently built between the wars was that motor buses could still operate profitably in new, less densely developed suburbs where passenger loadings would have been too low to justify building new tramways and railways. Another reason was that Town and Country Planning zoning introduced in new suburbs from 1909 onwards provided for different residential areas to be developed at varying densities, usually between four and twelve houses per acre. Plots in the middle zones were too small for detached houses but too large for terraces and therefore most suitable for semi-detached houses. The archetypal outer London semi may appear more prevalent than it really is because some developers erected semi-detached houses on the principal main road frontages but built terraces in the hinterland.

John Tarling, London SW15

The semi-detached houses identified by your correspondents are all far too modern. Here in Cornwall we have a pair of semis dating from the Roman occupation of Britain, in the second and third centuries AD. The stone-walled village of Chysauster near Penzance had the remains of a house that clearly takes the form of two semi-detached dwellings.

D. Stewart, Helston, Cornwall

I think Warwick can go one better than Blackheath,

Lancaster and Tottenham in that it can boast a pair of semi-detached houses that date from the late 1690s. The impressive building, which stands near the site of the old Northgate into the town, looks like one house, but is in fact two, divided by a central carriageway.

Amanda Clarke, Warwick

If a semi-detached house is one that was designed as a symmetrically arranged pair, there are several surviving examples in Coventry, dating back at least to the fourteenth century. Nos 169–70 Spon Street, Coventry, which was repaired under the supervision of the architect F. W. B. Charles in 1969–70 for the City of Coventry under the Spon Street Townscape scheme, is a good example of fourteenth-century date. Further along Spon Street is a sixteenth-century three-storey pair of town houses from 8–10 Much Park Street which was dismantled and reconstructed by Charles on its present site in 1971–4. Both these examples had houses built up against them, as the street frontage filled up and we feel sure that there must be many earlier examples that have become absorbed within later terraced development along urban streets. On the principle of originally detached, subsequently attached, we would be interested in hearing how common this type of 'semi' was in medieval towns.

George Demidowicz, conservation officer,
City of Coventry

Why is the control area of an aircraft called the cockpit?

A cockpit was a small dugout circle enclosed by wooden rails and used for cock-fighting, a popular seventeenth-century sport. Similar structures became to be called a cockpit by analogy: for example, the Cockpit Theatre, which would often feature bloody scenes on its confined stage.

Later, the back part of the orlop deck of a man-o'-war became known as the cockpit. It was narrow and deep, with wooden railings, and there was another connection with blood – during battle, wounded sailors were transferred to it. This opened up new meanings for cockpit linked to travel, while retaining the idea of a confined space.

In some ship designs the cockpit was also used for navigation. Travel in narrow, deep spaces was a feature of early aircraft. And the language of flying picked up many terms from seafaring – aeronautics, knots, navigation. So the 'cockpit' was borrowed to refer to the confined space in the fuselage for crew and passengers. Later it was specialized to mean the pilot's area.

Doug Gowan, London N8

Why does Britain's road system have so many

roundabouts? If they are such a good thing, why are they not so common in other countries?

The Netherlands used to have many roundabouts. The problem in the Netherlands and most continental countries is that traffic from the right has right of way (that would be from the left in Britain) unless one of the roads has an indicated priority. In the case of roundabouts, this leads to congestion: traffic entering the roundabout comes from the right and has right of way, which fills the roundabout but does not clear it. As a consequence, most Dutch roundabouts have been abolished. The British system works because traffic from the left does not have right of way and because traffic on a roundabout always has priority over the traffic approaching it.

Thomas van den Bergh, Tunbridge Wells, Kent

Traffic lights are more expensive.

Gordon Joly, London E14

The reason for having so many roundabouts in Britain is that our transport planning has been dominated by engineers obsessed with increasing the 'capacity' of the road system. Most other countries long realized that such features are major interruptions and extremely dangerous for the vulnerable road user such as cyclists.

Large sums of money are now being spent fitting signals.

Ironically, as well as improving safety, these also improve traffic flow, as the free-for-all at roundabouts in peak hours has now become a source of congestion in its own right.

Don Mathew, consultant on transport
and the environment, Lowestoft, Suffolk

If a Gents is closed, is there anything in law stopping me from nipping into the Ladies?

Some years ago, at a baseball stadium in Baltimore, a young woman in the long queue snaking out of the Ladies noticed that the Gents seemed empty. She nipped in – and was arrested, amid much media attention, for disturbing the peace. She went to court, sued the stadium for discrimination (since the number using the Ladies far outweighed those using the Gents) and won.

Jill Walden, Baltimore, Maryland

There will be a queue in the Ladies – don't bother!

Rachel Mear, Leicester

A refuse tip for Tendring council in Essex is directly opposite a holiday caravan camp called 'Shangri-La'. Do readers have other examples of inappropriate place or business names?

The funeral directors F. A. Holland & Son are based in Terminus Road, Littlehampton.

Bob Higham, Brighton

The Southern Water sewerage outfall to the east of Brighton leaves the shore at Portobello – the name was there before the sewers.

Bryan Moody, Hove, East Sussex

In Hemel Hempstead there is a small industrial estate called Paradise, and a business park called Dolittle Meadow.

Cecily Roberts, Hemel Hempstead, Herts

What are the determining factors that distinguish a hamlet from a village, a town and then a city? How does a settlement move up or down in status – e.g. through population size?

Our family has simple rules on this. Hamlet and village? The latter has a pub. Village or town? The latter has a Woolworth's.

R. Sanderson, Leamington Spa, Warks

The smallest settlement, a hamlet, is just a few houses, quite often around a farm. When in earlier times the hamlet increased in size and was deemed big enough to warrant its own priest, a church was built and it became a village. As the village grew and had sufficient farmers and traders to establish its own market, it became a town. When the town was of sufficient importance to warrant a cathedral or abbey, it became a city.

Peter Ward, Lansdown, Bath

In Britain there are no criteria that set out what a place is. For example, a town has to apply to the Queen to become a city and then on certain royal occasions the Queen decides to allow a couple of applications. Those that succeed and those that fail are never informed why.

Almost every other country has a clear process for identifying a city. In China, centuries of bureaucracy and civil service practice have arrived at highly detailed and inflexible criteria, including, for example, that the non-agricultural population of the town must exceed 120,000, of whom no fewer then 80,000 must be engaged in non-agricultural industries. By contrast, in the United States some states may label an area a city regardless of population size (Spring City, Tennessee has an approximate population of 2,000).

In Peru, criteria include population growth and the existence of educational institutions and hospitals. In Japan, rather differently, a city must have a population of 50,000 or more, and its inhabitants must be engaged in commercial or industrial pursuits. Thus, Tokyo contains several cities.

Once I moved a Ten Minute Rule Bill in the House of Commons to try to establish criteria for a place to become a city. The bill was one of many that died on their second reading.

Jane Griffiths MP, London SW1

In 1873, John Shortridge, an emigrant to North Carolina, remarked that the small cluster of houses surrounding his woollen mill at Mark's Creek would, in his native England, have been called a hamlet. 'This is not a hamlet yet,' he said, 'but I believe it will be one soon and perhaps in years to come a city; so we will name this tiny village hamlet and christen the baby town by planting a little tree.' The tree grew and so did the settlement, and with the rapid expansion of the railroads and attendant industries, the strategically placed Hamlet soon became a flourishing terminal for rail passengers and freight. By 1903 it had official city status and to the present day has enjoyed the distinction of being the City of Hamlet.

Gill Barker, Cambridge